1989

Women and Social Work

Towards a Woman-Centered Practice

Women and Social Work

Towards a Woman-Centered Practice

Jalna Hanmer

and

Daphne Statham

LYCEUM
BOOKS, INC.

224 S. Michigan Ave.
Chicago, IL 60604

This edition published by
LYCEUM BOOKS, INC.
224 S. Michigan Avenue
Chicago, Illinois 60604

First published in 1988 by
MACMILLAN EDUCATION LTD.
Houndmills, Basingstoke, Hampshire RG21 2XS and London

Library of Congress Cataloging-in-Publication Data

Hanmer, Jalna,
    Women and social work.

    Bibliography: p.
    Includes index.
    1. Social work with women—Great Britain. 2.Women
social workers—Great Britain. 3. Sexism—Great Britain.
I. Statham, Daphne. II. Title.
HV1448.G7H36 1989   362.8'3'0941   89-2356

LC card no. 89-2356

ISBN 0-925065-08-0

Cover design by Stuart D. Paterson. Printed and bound in the
United States by Malloy Lithographing, Inc.

Contents

Acknowledgements

Like all books this one is ascribed to particular authors. But while neither of us could have written it alone, neither could it have been written without the contribution of more than 100 women who attended the five Social Service Needs of Women courses between 1983 and 1985. Their names are listed on pp. ix–x. This is not a cosmetic attribution, but is an acknowledgement of how new practice theory is constructed. New developments in practice advance social work theory and come into being before they are conceptualised. Social Service Needs of Women courses provided an opportunity both for the course participants and for us to think through current practice and struggles in attempts to establish women centred social work.

After the draft of this book was written other women commented upon it and contributed to its further development. Claire Callender made a major contribution to Chapters 2 and 3. Reena Bhavnani, JoAn Saltzen, Sheila Saunders and Mary Harrison read drafts and made comments we have done our best to incorporate. Susan Noble typed various drafts of chapters with unfailing good humour and Mary Harrison helped in the completion of the bibliography. And finally, we wish to thank Jo Campling for her enthusiasm and support who, with Steve Kennedy, gently prodded us from time to time to complete a very overdue manuscript.

Daphne Statham is writing in her personal capacity.

JALNA HANMER
DAPHNE STATHAM

Nickie Armstrong
Lesley Baker
Sheila Baguley
Lynne Bailey
June Battye
Barbara Belcher
Eliza Benfield
Julie Brand
Isobel Bremner
Penny Brennan
Teresa Brill
Susan Brookman
Helen Brown
Susan Buchanan
Sandra Butler
Mary Cahill
Hilary Caldecott
Jill Carpenter
Elizabeth Chaloner
Lis Chance
Jan Clare
Penny Collier
Stella Collins
Mary Cousins
Cynthia Cole
Susan Crossley
Dorothy Degenhardt
Lise Dulniak
Eunice Dunkley
Sarah Durham
Pem Ellis
Mary Evans
Edna Feenan
Annette Fleming
Annie Fletcher
Angela Forrest
Sue Francomb

Bridget Gates
Moira Gavin
Carol Gibbons
Rosalind Gill
Penny Grant
Annette Gurney
Susan Hanks
Marjorie Hummond
Linda Hartley
Nicky Heseltine
Marilyn Hodge
Bronwen Holden
Wendy Holmes
Joy Howard
Evelyn Hunter
Marie Johnson
Susan Kay
Anne Kendall
Lesley Kettles
Sue Kirk
Sheilia Killick
Pat King
Mary Langan
Sandra Lester
Sally Lloyd
Trish Lloyd
Yvonne Lloyd
Lesley Long
Francis Lowe
Janet Lyon
Annette Martin
Chris Mason
Pauline McCourt
Hedi McGee
Elaine McKenzie
Virginia McLernon
Roisin McManus

Jill McMurray
Diana McNeish
Maureen McPhail
Hilary Matthews
Wanda Mendoza
Fiona Merritt
Victoria Mole
Katherine Murphy Jones
Jan Nairn
Peggy Parry
Kathryn Peart
Anne Peasland
Pat Price
Rosie Rae
Sue Raikes
Noreen Randle
Stella Redgrave
Helen Reeves
Susan Ridding

Megan Rhys
Vivien Shah
Jayne Shakespeare
Sue Stanworth
Irene Starr
Moira Strutt
Janine Stewart
Joyce Thom
Jennifer Twelvetrees
Susan Walker
Amorer Wason
Hazel Waldron
Pat Walton
Diane Watson
Aileen West
Laura Williams
Cathy Wood
Nicola Woodward

Introduction

In 1952, Simone de Beauvoir wrote that women "lacked concrete means for organizing themselves into a unit. . . . They have no past, no history, no religion of their own; and they have no . . . solidarity of work and interest. . ."* Almost forty years have passed since those words were written and much has changed for individual woman. Yet the patriarchal institutions and social structures that shape our policies and behavior remain firmly in place, and women continue to be defined more by their roles in relation to men than by their individual identity as women. Feminist scholars theorize that divisiveness is fostered, impeding women's understanding of the essential commonalities among women. Efforts are well underway to reclaim women's past, women's history, and yes, even women's religion, but the core of the theme that would "organize women into a unit" while respecting our infinite diversity continues to elude us.

The profession of social work is a microcosm of the society that supports and legitimates it. Thus, we should expect concerned women to reflect the conflicts and contradictions embedded in the larger society. These conflicts and contradictions may, in fact, be heightened by the fact that social work is commonly characterized as a woman's profession; a majority both of clients and workers are women. Ironically, the societal mandate to those who deliver social services is to control and monitor the prescribed behavior of women so that they will better fulfill their roles as wives, mothers, daughters, carers. The profession all too often accedes to such mandates, which violate its humanistic values.

The women's movement has provided the impetus for reexamination of the way women have fared in social work. The subordinate role of women as professionals and the damage done to women as clients are by this time well documented. Much scholarship has been devoted to defining problems and to building new theory and knowledge to redress past wrongs and to forge a new practice of empowerment. Operationalizing and gaining wide acceptance for non-sexist and feminist practice is proving to be a long and arduous process.

This is the task undertaken in *Women and Social Work*. The British Association of Social Work sponsored a series of courses on the social service needs of women over a four-year period. The 111 participants were stimulated to reframe their views of themselves as women social workers and their view of their women clients. They did this by examining the significance of the commonalities and differences they identified between themselves and their clients. This volume explains and synthesizes the social workers' struggles to understand and conceptualize the meaning of what they learned. It conveys to readers practical ways to implement a client-centered practice that recognizes gender.

Women and Social Work questions and ultimately rejects the control and monitor mandate mentioned above. Rethinking and redefining the problems of social service delivery led the social workers to a radically altered search for solutions. The basic claim of the book is that gender is a profound influence in social work and that its relevance has been neither acknowledged nor understood. Moreover, the relationship between women workers and their clients transcends the helper–helpee dimension, encompassing powerful dynamics that must be recognized. These dynamics have to do with the commonalities all women share by virtue of existing in the same society; and also with the divergences to be expected as a result of differences of class, race, education, economic condition, and life experience. Parenthetically, it is of equal importance for men in social work who work with women clients and colleagues to become informed about these new perspectives.

These themes have been presented before; American social workers of a feminist persuasion will find them familiar. Yet frequently we find a glass wall between practice wisdom and research studies. *Women and Social Work* should suggest fruitful opportunities for practitioners and researchers to reinforce and extend one another's learnings—often a difficult undertaking. The singular contribution of *Women and Social Work* is to begin with the real-life experiences of the social workers and their clients, interweaving insights in a way that forces us to reexamine conventional wisdom about women and poverty, dependency, caring, relations with men, etc.

This book is a rich resource for practice. Social workers in training will find in its pages much to ponder and much to help shape their developing professional selves. Feminist literature in social work provides the basis for the workers who participated in the courses to break down the false dichotomies and artificial separations between themselves and their clients. But the thrust of the book is on how-to—how to understand, how to work with, how to change one's own perceptions, how to put into operation a woman-centered practice. A side benefit is the opportunity to compare social services for women as offered in a different country—one with similar, but not identical, organization of services. The practicing social worker, interested in expanding insights and skills in working with women, but not well-grounded in feminist approaches, will also benefit from *Women and Social Work*.

Both Great Britain and the United States in recent years have been governed by administrations espousing social policies that women have found detrimental to their interests. Beyond reforming personal social services, *Women and Social Work* advocates direct action by women to change social policies. Women must take charge of empowering themselves, however slow and halting progress may be. We are called upon to improve ourselves, to mobilize, and to make common cause with our clients because our cause *is* a common one. Only thus will we move at last toward achieving the solidarity of interest that was part of Simone de Beauvoir's vision for women so many years ago.

Betty Sancier, Professor
School of Social Welfare,
University of Wisconsin-Milwaukee,
and Editor-in-Chief,
AFFILIA *Journal of Women and Social Work*

*Simone de Beauvoir, *The Second Sex*, translated and edited by H. M. Parshley (NY: Vintage Books, 1974), p. xxii.

Preface: Why Write a Book on Women and Social Work?

The way we conceptualise and define our problems has everything to do with the solutions we seek (Morell, 1981, p. 39).

This book is about reframing the relevance of gender to social work. The focus is on women as social workers and clients for two reasons. Firstly, the contradictions and paradoxes that govern women's lives are ill understood by social work educators and in social work practice. The adverse effect this lack of understanding has on social work practice with women is the second reason for focusing on women as workers and clients. Women have a higher risk than men of becoming clients of social services and a lower risk of becoming clients of probation. But in both situations women are vulnerable to less than adequate practice.

Gender is a total experience for women. Social work practice defines women as wives, mothers, carers, adolescent girls, i.e. in relation to their sexual behaviour, and not as people. But paradoxically gender is invisible. When confronted, for example, with a physically handicapped or elderly woman, linguistically, women disappear into the categoric 'family' or 'informal carers'. These are euphemisms for major forms of social work practice with women.

Who depends on who—is a question of fundamental relevance to understanding the paradoxes and contradictions in the lives of women. Are women dependent on men, psychologically and socially, or are men dependent on women? Or is the question of dependence much more subtle and complicated? For example, women look to men for protection from violence, yet it is men who are the most likely source of violence to women. The closer the relationship between men and women, the more likely women are to be abused. It is illogical for women to look to the men with whom they live for protection as these are the very men most likely to physically and sexually assault them. But this too, is hidden.

Caring for others is equally problematic. Caring for others, whether husbands, children, aged parents or someone else, makes women financially and socially dependent on individual men or the state. Yet at the same time it is children, men and other dependent adults who are psychologically, and often socially and financially, dependent on women. But this reverse dependency is invisible; hidden within an ideology that defines women as dependents of men.

To reframe the dependency of women as founded on the dependence of others upon them is to reveal a more complex and valid truth. This understanding of dependency is the result of the work and analysis of women over the past two decades. Other authors present well-thought-out and considered positions about the role of women and feminity which differ radically from those advanced in this text. The aim may be to counter the views of that broad grouping called 'the Women's Movement', of which we have been part, by presenting women as being truly fulfilled only through marriage and motherhood (Scruton, 1980; Mount, 1982; Anderson and Dawson, 1986).

This book is the result of six short courses, five with women only and one with men only. Over a four-year period courses on The Social Service Needs of Women took place in both the North and South of England. The first course offered by the National Institute of Social Work in 1983 was repeated in 1984 and 1985. Lancashire Social Services Department offered the course in 1983 and Leeds Social Services Department followed in 1985 with two courses, one for women only and the other for men only. A total of 111 women participated, drawn primarily from field social work, but also day care, residential and community work. Both social services and probation workers took part.

We are deeply indebted to the insights, practical work and struggles of women social workers. The practice of some of the women who attended the Social Services Needs of Women courses is in advance of current social work theory and literature although there is a growing concern with gender issues in social work education and practice (Ahmed, 1985; Association of Community Workers, 1982; Ball, 1985; Brook and Davis, 1985; Burden and Gottlieb 1987; Currer, 1984; Dale and Foster, 1986; Davis, 1985; Dominelli, 1986; Ernst and Goodison, 1981; Fernando, 1984; Fritze, 1982; Garvin and Reed, 1983; Goldner, 1985; Gottlieb, 1980, 1983; Hale, 1983; Hanmer, 1979; Hare-Mustin, 1978; Howell and Bayer, 1981; Hudson, 1985; Lawrence, 1984; McLeod and Dominelli, 1982; Mander and Rush, 1974; Marchant and Wearing, 1986; Mayo, 1977; Morrell, 1981; 1987; Nairne and Smith, 1984; Numa, 1985; Osborne, 1983; Pennell and Allen, 1984; Statham, 1978; Walton, 1975; Wilkinson, 1986; Wilson, 1977, 1980; Wise, 1985). The problems women workers face in conveying to others their understanding of the lives of women clients and the need for a client-centred practice that recognises gender were explored and developed. The focus was on how to move forward positively. We see this book as a shared collaborative venture with the women who took part in the short courses, and with you the reader. We hope you will respond to these ideas and experiences by developing them further through your own practice.

Our primary intention is to make women visible as clients and as workers. This involves a restructuring of thought and values; women must become valued in and for themselves. Making women visible also involves a greater understanding of the conflicts experienced by women, and the demands made upon them, both as clients and as workers. It also involves challenging current thinking about client groups and types of problems facing social workers.

The ultimate aim is to facilitate assessment and planning so that non-sexist women-centred practice can emerge. This involves taking into account both individual and institutional sexism. Sexism can be expressed consciously or unconsciously through individual relationships, in groups, and through organisational practice and policies. Institutional sexism is the structuring of power and privilege within organisations so that one sex, by virtue of its sex, occupies a superior position. It may seem as if individuals have nothing to do with the 'way things are'. The system may appear to operate without reference to the individuals or groups that make it up. Both those who benefit and those who do not may feel powerless to intervene in the processes that maintain a system of inequality, and even oppression.

We see the presentation of an alternative view on women and their problems as the first crucial step in the emergence of non-sexist women-centred practice. In the following chapters we attempt to weave together a woman-centred perspective on women, both as clients and as workers, with suggestions on how to begin to realise women-centred practice. The major objective is to show how a gendered approach to social work will more effectively serve the needs and wishes of women clients and women workers and, in this way, social work organisations and people generally.

The perspective includes a recognition of diversities between women as well as commonalities. In locating diversities between women based on race, country of origin, and religious background, we use the terms as defined by the Inner London Education Authority in 'A Policy for Equality: Race' (1983):

- Afro-Caribbean refers to people whose origins are in Africa or the Caribbean.
- Asian refers to people whose origins are in the Indian Subcontinent.
- Black refers to both Afro-Caribbean and Asian people. The terms black emphasises the common experience which both Afro-Caribbean and Asian people have of being victims of racism and their common determination to oppose racism.
- Ethnic minorities refers to other groups who, together with the black communities, suffer varying degrees of prejudice and discrimination. The ILEA document speci-

fies Chinese, Greek Cypriots, Turkish Cypriots, Turks, Vietnamese, Moroccans, Irish, and Jews. While providing a list they make it clear that, like ourselves, there is no intention to exclude any minority group.

1

Commonalities and Diversities between Women Clients and Women Social Workers

Racism, the belief in the inherent superiority of one race over all others and thereby the right to dominance. Sexism, the belief in the inherent superiority of one sex over the other and thereby the right to dominance. Ageism, Heterosexism, Elitism, Classism.

'It is a lifetime pursuit for each one of us to extract these distortions from our living at the same time as we recognize, reclaim, and define those differences upon which they are imposed. For we have all been raised in a society where those distortions were endemic within our living. Too often, we pour the energy needed for recognizing and exploring difference into pretending those differences are insurmountable barriers, or that they do not exist at all. This results in a voluntary isolation, or false and treacherous connections. Either way, we do not develop tools for using human difference as a springboard for creative change within our lives. We speak not of human difference, but of human deviance' (Lorde, 1984, pp. 115–16).

We are not accustomed or trained to think about commonalities and diversities between ourselves and our clients as a rich resource for practice. To be useful for practice, commonality and diversity have to be re-recognised and re-conceptualised. This is necessary because commonalities can be confused with sameness, and diversities can be confused with traditionally drawn boundaries between clients and workers.

Generic issues

As we all know, client groups are the elderly, children and young people, the mentally and physically handicapped, ethnic minorities, the delinquent and criminal. Attention is focussed on certain aspects of problems while ignoring other areas of commonalities between the individuals contained within these classifications. For example, most clients are working class and poor, but these are not the commonalities around which social work practice and services are organised (Jones, 1983). Similarly, gender is excluded as means of categorising the people who use social services.

There is no particular logic in excluding from social work classifications the categories adults, women, men, the poor and unemployed, except that client groups are those categories for which the state has accepted overtly some responsibility for their care and control. These responsibilities are formalised through the statutes relating to social services and probation. Yet they do not necessarily make sense as a way of categorising people to those outside social work. For instance, physical handicap is a meaningless grouping to an anthropologist (Oliver, 1983), and community groups are more likely to find common cause around such issues as poverty, housing, unemployment, racism, women, or neighbourhood.

The idea of gender as a significant dimension in social work is not a new one. Kadushin as long ago as 1976 stated that gender issues are embedded in the profession and service delivery. Even using existing client categories, specific problems, such as drug use or offending behaviour by women, involve returning to the position of women in society (Gottlieb, 1980; Garvin and Reed, 1983).

Commonalities

Women social workers and clients share commonalities. They group around being female, their relationships with men, children, living within the nuclear family, employment possibilities and working conditions, and more general cultural expectations and pressures on women. These commonalities offer both a resource and a strength for practice. We suggest that it is only through a recognition of commonalities that a true assessment of the situation facing women clients and a client-centred practice can emerge.

In social work there is no stress on commonality between social workers and clients. We come across commonalities more by accident than as part of our formal training and education. We can feel surprise, shock, shame and denial. To recognise commonalities is thought to raise the danger of over-identification, of over-emotional involvement, thereby producing an inability to respond to the clients' problems 'objectively'. This can negate important commonalities like gender, class, age, race, sexuality, culture and other differentiating characteristics between people.

Although increasingly there is teaching about women on basic courses in sociology, social administration and psychology, there is much less emphasis on gender within teaching on social work practice whether in college or agency. Here the day-to-day lives of women take place as if in a vacuum, set apart in a world of social work methods and skills. Insights to be gained from the context and day-to-day experiences of women are dimly perceived and under-used when social worker and client meet. Similarly scant attention is paid as to how this material connects with the lives of social workers or students themselves.

The capacity to become self-aware is valued in social work. Understanding ourselves, our values and attitudes, and the impact our style of work has on others is regarded as an important part of training and professional development. Recognising and understanding gendered experience, however, is largely ignored as an important element in developing self-awareness.

Discussions on self-disclosure are equally gender-blind.

While the merits and demerits of self-disclosure are frequently discussed in the literature on counselling and interviewing (Sutton, 1979), gender, like being black or age, is not something we can choose when or where to disclose. It is not a matter of working at the client's pace or, for that matter, our own. It is visible from first contact.

We believe that the social service needs of women cannot be discussed until we become aware of the commonalities between our lives and the lives of our women clients. In contrast with the emphasis on difference prevalent in much training and supervision on the job, the women on the Social Service Needs of Women courses were quick to identify what they had in common with their clients. There were a number of key commonalities arising from basic life experiences which we explore in the following chapters. These are:

1. The problematic impact on women of female life experience.
2. The public-private division of life through managing the double load of home and paid work.
3. Women's relationships with men and the impact on our private and public worlds.
4. Being mothers and caring for dependents generally.
5. Women's relationships with women.
6. The influence, more generally, of society on women.

An alliance developed over the life of the courses between the participants and the invisible clients. It was not one of 'collusion' or of 'over-involvement', but one that recognised commonalities:

between client and worker
between women workers
between women irrespective of age, stage, sexuality, class, race, reproductive history.

These commonalities existed whether or not the women concerned were wives or mothers, carers of dependent adults, or in paid employment.

In making the commonalities we share as women conscious, visible parts of our practice we learn that we need not, and indeed must not, be ashamed or surprised by them but incorporate them into our work. One way to bring commonalities into the open in our thinking and planning is to make them explicit in some way, for instance, beginning with the individual or collective drawing up a list. We can then build on it and revise it as our lives change and develop thereby making the recognition of commonalities a conscious part of our practice.

For men the task is different. They need to find ways of drawing into their conscious practice what they see as commonalities between women in an effort to move towards a more sophisticated understanding of gender. A move is required from stereotypical assumptions and responses such as: 'typical woman', 'just like a woman', 'can't trust a woman', towards a deeper understanding and perception of the lives and experiences of women clients and colleagues. It then becomes possible for male social workers to examine the impact of their behaviour towards colleagues. Equally important for male workers whose work is primarily with women is to translate these understandings into practice. Men can also begin to identify attitudes and behaviour towards male clients and colleagues whose work or family situations involve them in tasks usually carried out by women. Men need to learn to be comfortable with gender deviance and diversity amongst themselves.

Diversities

Diversities exist between the same categories of women:

between clients
between women workers
between women generally

Diversities, however, are frequently not readily apparent except in stereotypical ways. The task of identification requires conscious deliberation and gives rise to questions such as: Are power relations basic to diversity? Who decides what is a diversity between women? What is the significance of diversities? For example, how do race or class or gender or the expression of sexuality interact? Are these diversities natural qualities or socially determined attributes? All are important questions to which there are no easy or simple answers. They need debate and discussion; there will be disagreement and conflict. Over time we may change our minds because of new experience or knowledge, but it is important to make these opinions part of our conscious assessment and plans.

Employment

Employment was identified as a diversity of major importance on the courses. Professional status brings social workers as opposed to women clients a higher earning capacity and equal pay, greater access to education and training, better conditions of work, and a job which allows greater flexibility to plan and organise work. Adequate pay gives social workers access to decent housing, transport, and opens up options for women generally.

Some women social workers have difficulties returning to work after a period away, for example after the birth of a child. The problems experienced are unlikely to be as great as those facing many of their working-class women clients. Some who want to return to work after caring for children or dependent relatives have a period of unemployment, as do women who are tied to a particular geographical area because of their husband's work, or who have inadequate child-care arrangements. But unemployment is not, at least at the date of writing, a major problem in social work, although it can be an experience women social workers share with other women workers.

Unlike social workers, most women clients will be in workplaces where there is occupational segregation of men and women. In a survey of women's employment carried out in 1981, 63 per cent of women worked in jobs done only by women at their place of work. Further, 'There was a clear realisation . . . that if men were not doing these jobs it was likely to be because they were not prepared to do them, usually because the work was women's work and or the pay was too low' (Martin and Roberts, 1984b, p. 204). In the same survey, 81 per cent of the women's husbands worked only alongside men, where the pay and often the conditions of employment were better.

Black and white women

The different experiences of black and white women were another source of diversity identified on the courses. The recognition of diversities is particularly acute when black clients meet white social workers and black social workers meet white clients. Combining gender differences with race intensifies diversity; for example, white women clients with black men social workers or black women clients with white men social workers (Bhavnani, 1987). Black social workers also experience a status contradiction from being black and holding power as a social worker (Harrison, 1987).

The day-to-day lives of poor black and poor white women within the family, combining paid work with domestic labour and caring for children and dependent adults were commonalities. However, racism means that black women have to live with a sharper sense of the contradiction that the family is both oppressive to them and at the same time a source of support. For black women, the family is a refuge from racism. For a number of black people immigration controls mean separation from their children and husbands, wives and fiancé(e)s. The aim is to unite the members of the family (Cohen, 1980; Cohen and Siddiqi, 1985; Women, Immigration and Nationality Group, 1985).

The recognition of commonalities and the easy develop-ment of companionship between black and white women is restricted by the knowledge of the power white women hold. Black women describe the conditions they have to place on their feelings and commitment to white women, almost like having to 'hedge your bets', because racism could intervene at any time. 'White women are born with it [power] and the greater their economic privilege the greater their power' (Moraga and Anzaldua, 1981, p. 62); or again, 'Within the community of women, racism is a reality force within my life as it is not within yours.' (Lorde, 1981, p. 97). The continuing struggle to identify this imbalance of power and the effects it has on racism between women has fallen mainly on black women.

It is for this reason that Audre Lorde 'decided never again to speak to white women about racism. I felt it was wasted energy, because of their destructive guilt and defensiveness, and because whatever I had to say might better be said by white women to one another, at far less emotional cost to the speaker and probably a better hearing.' A letter to Mary Daly broke this silence (Lorde, 1981). Audre Lorde pointed out that black women have a past in which their foremothers, mythological and real, played a prominent role.

Recognising commonalities means understanding that there are areas in which black women's struggles and issues are different from those of white women. In action a black woman may decide to prioritise being black. In terms of her experience, however, being black and being a woman are hard to separate (Bhavnani, 1987). Black women are acutely conscious of the discriminatory way black men are treated at their places of work, on the streets, and by the criminal justice system. Both in the UK (Home Office, 1986) and in the USA (Burden and Gottleib, 1987) the construction of black men as abusers, aggressive criminals and rapists feeds into the power of white people and, in our view, particularly that of white men.

Black women also are acutely conscious that their children are disadvantaged in schools by racism. The family is an important means by which black women and men, children and young people, can gain a positive image of themselves and avoid the powerlessness that comes from the negative valuation placed on them by external sources. Further, the dynamics of racism are not well understood by white women. Decisions to prioritise gender for black women are mediated by this knowledge (Bryan *et al.*, 1985; Feminist Review, 1984; Lorde 1981, 1984; Solomon, 1976; Walker, 1984; Wilson, 1978).

Feeling powerful–feeling powerless

Women clients and social workers do not meet as equals, and in focusing on commonalities we must not forget the power differences between social worker and client. But this is not a simple dichotomy, although the powerful statutory social worker versus the powerless women clients is a theme in many discussions. A second way in which a power–powerlessness dichotomy is organised is to experience oneself, a woman social worker, as powerless and the agency as powerful. Although we all feel like this at times, in relation both to clients and organisational structures, a crude division of powerful–powerless is an oversimplification. This is so both in a general sense when thinking in categories, i.e. clients and social workers, social workers and organisations, and when considering the relationships of specific clients with specific social workers or individual social workers with individual line managers.

There was an emphasis on the powerless of clients on the courses which may be partly explained by the high representation of field workers in relation to community workers. Field work, because of its focus on individual pathology, problems and failures, has been and still is more concerned with clients' weaknesses. In contrast, community work emphasises mobilising resources and strengths in collectivities and within the individuals who belong to them (Mayo, 1977; Association of Community Workers, 1982; Fritze, 1982).

However, the emphasis on the powerlessness of women clients was so total that they were never described as better off than women social workers, although in some individual and group situations this may be so, in some respects if not totally. There are disadvantages in being a professional social worker not necessarily shared by clients. These include the inability to acknowledge publicly any sexuality but heterosexuality; the difficulty in acknowledging some political opinions and activities, or lifestyles that deviate from the hetereosexual, nuclear family and, for black social workers, being a representative of the state, particularly when conflict between black communities and the state increases, for example as in recent years in Brixton, Toxteth, Bristol, Tottenham and Handsworth.

Social workers are mostly seen as powerful, and clients as powerless, although in reality many of the disadvantages in clients' lives may be experienced by women social workers. There are a number of bases for exploring this powerful–powerless dichotomy. The first arises out of a focus on life opportunities and experiences associated with social class. Guilt arising from the advantages brought by professional occupation can create social distance from clients and the ignoring of commonalities between women.

A second base compares groups of women in relation to men. For example, who is more oppressed in her personal relationships, the middle-class woman social worker or the working-class woman client? Gender and class interact in complex ways and social workers have the same problems in their relationships with men as do clients. For example, some of us have been sexually abused, others have been, or are, in violent relationships with men. The worker may move from being confident and powerful in her work to being less in control of her life at home and/or to face problems similar to those of the clients she has been working with during the day.

A third representation of the powerful–powerless dichotomy between women is in relation to economic resources, but again this is not straightforward. Many middle-class women would be unable to maintain their economic class on their own. Their husbands' incomes are essential to their class position. Further, even when women earn, they may not have control over their incomes. This is true for both middle-/ and working-class women (Homer, Leonard and Taylor, 1984; Pahl, 1980, 1982). Most of the social workers on our courses enjoyed higher wages than their clients, but a number from working-class origins who had only recently qualified knew they would have to go onto social security, or become dependent on men again, if wages were not paid during the disputes about fixing of the rates which were then occurring in some London boroughs.

A fourth representation is based on age. Powerfulness and powerlessness affect women of any age, but in a society where youth is valued and identified with vigour, beauty and creativity, ageing brings specific difficulties (McDonald and Rich, 1984). There is a danger that the richness of women's lives will be ignored (Hemmings, 1985). Also, women are expected to look after others, not to be cared for, but the older one becomes the more likely it is that personal care will be needed.

A fifth representation of the powerful–powerless dichotomy between women is in relation to being black, belonging to an ethnic minority group, and racism. Black women experience the powerlessness associated with racism, but black women social workers face racism both from clients, and the more subtle racism of their colleagues and the organisations in which they work.

Sexuality is a sixth difference between women described as dividing between into the powerful and powerless. Because of homophobia, heterosexual women are seen as powerful and lesbian women as powerless. In these last two differences it was particularly noticeable that only the women on the courses who had directly experienced racism and/or homophobia were fully aware of the damage this does to women.

Awareness of differences arises out of direct experience and sharing what we learn with and from each other. There is a danger that in a predominantly white, heterosexual, able-bodied and middle-class work-force certain differences are given more attention than others. Income, relationships with men, and education are emphasised rather than disability, race, ethnic minority memberships, lesbianism, or age.

We suggest that how *this* particular woman's situation and problems differ from one's own should become a part of assessment. Differences in status, power, role, lifestyle, race, culture, sexuality, education, work possibilities, access to community resources, degree of stigma and hope, are elements in the differentiation of social worker from client. But how is the recognition of diversities aided by the recognition of similarities?

Recognising diversity through commonality

Recognising commonalities affects the approach of the social worker. While it may appear paradoxical, recognising commonalities gives the social worker the psychological distance necessary to see the client in her setting. The worker is given both the personal space and the theoretical perspective to enable her to recognise how the forces of society in general and of personal relationships in particular affect the client's emotional and practical responses.

Without a process of recognising first commonalities and then differences, the danger of stereotyping women clients as the 'not coping' and social workers as the 'coping' is far greater. This process of psychological distancing results in objectifying the woman client; seeing her in terms of social roles rather than as a person in her own right. The recognition of the woman's own strength, powers and her ability to solve problems, is inhibited. There can be a lack of contact rather than a reflective response.

The greater insight that comes from the recognition of diversities in the context of commonality is rooted in genuine contact with and perception of the other person. Social workers who are open to this process and knowledge are less likely to impose either their own stereotypes or their personal solutions onto women clients. They will be able to make an assessment focussed on the woman and on women clients, and will be more likely to facilitate groups for women who have common life experiences. The empowerment they offer woman clients individually and collectively extends to themselves. They are less likely to despair within themselves; to see themselves silently and secretly as the only social worker who is 'not coping' amongst all their amazonian colleagues. They possess the potential to break through the definition of reality for women workers and clients which is portrayed by the cartoon showing women in little box-like flats in a tower block surrounded by dirty dishes and children asking 'Why can't I cope?', while the social worker in the nearby single rise office surrounded by mounds of paper asks 'Why can't I cope?'. This powerlessness can be broken by practice which makes the recognition of commonalities its cornerstone.

Recognising commonalities encourages empathy and avoids responses that arise from victim blaming. Empathy facilitates the acknowledgement of the lack of choices for women. It inhibits the 'you ought' response, however covert. For example, recognising that difficulties in relationships with men are a part of many lives focuses attention and practice on how the client can gain more support from other women. The acknowledgement of shared health issues focuses attention on how to help the client reduce and deal with stress. Recognising that women are oppressed as women creates reality in the social worker's approach.

The organisation of service, of teaching and learning, does not facilitate the recognition of generic themes in relation to women clients, or in the relationship between women social workers and women clients. This is a major deficiency in social work practice theory. The significance of gender can be grouped under three main headings based on women's unequal access to economic and social resources.

1. *Women as carers*

Women are defined in relation to the roles they perform for men, children and other relatives. They have a career as carers (Finch and Groves, 1983). Women are usually defined as the responsible parent in one-/and two-parent families. In practice there are no expectations regarding fatherhood, not even in respect of family income, as social security is readily accepted as a substitute if fathers refuse to contribute to their families (Land, 1976, 1978, 1983, 1986).

Parenting means mothering
This is best illustrated by the extreme case, even if it is seen as bad practice within social work. Fathers, biological or social, who abuse their children may never, or rarely, be seen in subsequent monitoring of children's progress by social workers. The mother will be seen and held responsible

for ensuring that the children are not abused again. Even when father is seen, the emphasis is on monitoring mother's care.

Similarly, the care of dependent adults is seen primarily as the responsibility of women. Expectations of the level, regularity and duration of care is higher for women than for men. A son, husband or father may be condemned for not visiting regularly enough, but praised for keeping up weekly visits or doing the shopping. A woman in the same position is expected, and will expect of herself, much more than this before she is awarded public approbation as a 'good' wife, daughter, mother. Different valuations are placed on caring behaviour, depending on the gender of the carer.

2.   *Women as subordinates to men*

Women as carers of men have a special quality in that the services women perform are not recognised as such. Women in relation to men are seen as dependents who are cared for. The washing, cooking, cleaning, nursing, entertaining, etc., that women do for men become invisible. The lack of reciprocity is ignored. Women here are not carers, but social subordinates: labour is a right, a gift that cannot be recognised or counted in assessing the nature of the relationship. Failure to comply with these unrecognised labour requirements become a justification for maltreatment (Chapter 5). To expose these expectations, substitute the picture of the elderly parent and son for the wife who is regrettably hit by her husband if, say his dinner is not on the table on time (Maynard, 1985). This excuse would be more likely to be seen as inadequate and bizarre if offered by a son for an attack on an elderly mother. The recognition of differential responses by social workers, such as in this example, exposes institutionalised sexism.

3.   *Women and personal identity*

All the specific new approaches to women, in response for

example to depression or drug or alcohol abuse, treat *identity* in women as crucial in overcoming the specific symptom of distress (Gottlieb, 1980; Burden and Gottlieb, 1987). Women report a lack of self-esteem, feelings of worthlessness in many life experiences. Why is this? Is this the place to begin, or at least an aspect of women's problems that should never be ignored, if genuine progress is to be made with women?

We develop these themes in the following chapters, beginning with women's life patterns and the context in which women live.

Questions

1. (i) What do you think you have in common with other women?
    (ii) How do you think you differ from other women?
2. What do you think are the most important ways in which women clients are (i) worse off (ii) better off than woman social or community workers?
3. Can you think of social or community situations in which you feel powerful? Can you think of social or community work situations in which you feel powerless? What factors contribute to these experiences?
4. What do you think are the major advantages and disadvantages of being a social or community worker?
5. Think of work with a woman client. Does her situation differ from your own? How is it similar? Have you made these factors a part of your assessment in planning how to intervene?
6. Think of two black women. In what ways are their situations different and similar? Do the differences and similarities you have identified apply to you?

2

Women, Dependency and Poverty

with Claire Callender

To make woman-centred assessments and plans social workers need:

1. to acquire information about women and their life patterns, including knowledge of the policies that may apply to women and the services women use and
2. to develop an awareness of assumptions which serve to structure the assessment of individuals and groups of women.

Social workers rarely work solely with a client in a one-to-one relationship. The vast majority of work involves liaison with other people inside and outside our own agency. This happens because of the way the welfare state is organised and because many of the problems clients bring to social workers are complex, with multiple, not single, causes necessitating the intervention or resources of more than one person or agency. The task of getting more woman-centred assessments and practice is, therefore, much larger than changing ourselves and our own agencies.

The question is how to begin. Often we, and those we must work with on behalf of women clients, are unaware of the frameworks being used to structure social work theory and practice. These frameworks may be invisible, yet they determine what is seen, heard, and considered important (Penfold and Walker, 1984).

The paradox faced by social workers is that while women are the primary clients of social service departments, of many voluntary and private agencies, women are not recognised as a legitimate group in social work. There are no statutory responsibilities to women as a group as, for example, there are for children and the elderly. When a child or an elderly person is abused social workers are required by statute to act. With abused women social work decisions are of a different order. The social worker who acts in such cases may be deemed culpable of undue haste or of breaking up a marriage. This criticism is far less likely to occur in relation to children or elderly people.

The process of response is socially constructed in a way that makes the process of learning about women and applying knowledge of them in a conscious way difficult. Knowledge about women is not structured to make it easier to use. On social work courses gender is frequently banished from social work practice teaching into the territories of the contributory disciplines of psychology, sociology and social policy. Assumptions and prejudices about women remain unchallenged. To influence practice and policy directly, information about women needs organising in ways that can be translated readily into the assessment and planning process and then into action.

To work effectively with women, it is vital to develop frameworks that do not pathologise the behaviour of individuals and groups of women simply because they do not fit rigid categories of 'what ought to be'. Through information about the life patterns of women and the context in which women live we can begin to unmesh the tangle caused by confusing social and demographic changes in the lives of women with social problems and/or individual deviancy or pathology. By understanding women's life patterns we can recognise problems which are being denied through the way services and policies are structured as well as recognise assumptions about the correctness or inevitability of certain stereotypical roles for women.

Women's life patterns

If we look at women's lives over the life cycle, we see that women experience more than one pattern of living. Women often begin life in a one-/ or two-parent nuclear family. They may marry directly or after a short time of living alone or in some more collective setting with other women and men. The marriage is more likely to result in children than not and many women spend some time as a single parent or again as a single person. Most divorced women remarry, although a significant proportion do not. Finally at the end of her life a woman may spend a few years alone again or with other adults to whom she may or may not be related. Married women, like single women or married men, may have relationships with their own or the opposite sex while remaining married.

These patterns are not 'abnormal' or even undesirable in and of themselves. It is the social valuation and expectations that we place on people that result in negative value judgments. The actual lives of women are deviating more and more from the cultural ideal in the past and from that being asserted today by the New Right both here and in the USA (Levitas, 1986). This point is important when making assessments in social work as the trends we will identify are likely to continue.

A variety of patterns of living, either on a permanent or temporary basis, are the experience of an increasing number of people. Trends particularly relevant for social workers to consider are:

1. The increasing number of one-parent families. This is the family form for one out of every eight adults with dependent children (*Social Trends*, 1986, p. 33).
2. The increasing number of couples who have a period of living together before they marry. By the late 1970s about 26 per cent (Study Commission on the Family, 1983, p. 11).
3. The increasing number of men and women who experience serial monogamy; that is, marriage, divorce and remarriage. The estimate is that one in three marriages

will end in divorce. Approximately 80 per cent of people under 30 will remarry within a few years (Study Commission on the Family, 1983). This means that one in three marriages are re-marriages for one of the partners while for one in six both will be remarriages.

4. The continued reduction in the number of people occupying households. In 1984 only 33 per cent of households had children under 16 years (*Social Trends,* 1986, p. 32).

5. The increasing number of married women with children who are in employment. More than 50 per cent of women with dependent children are economically active (Study Commission on the Family, 1983, p. 17; Martin and Roberts, 1984a, 1984b). Employment patterns have changed so greatly that the man as sole breadwinner supporting a wife and two children is representative of only 8 per cent of the male workforce and, if working women are included, 5 per cent the total workforce (Study Commission on the Family 1983, p.19). Paid employment is now the norm for women (Martin and Roberts, 1984b, p. 200).

6. The increasing overt challenge to heterosexuality as the only valid form of sexual relationship and way of life (Rich, 1980). We do not know the statistical significance of this, but many women are more open about their relationships with other women given a slightly more positive social climate than in the past. A figure of one in ten is often cited as the proportion of women who have made a primary attachment to women rather than men (Kinsey *et al.*, 1953; Rights of Women Lesbian Custody Group, 1986). A few women choose to live with other women in preference to living with men or alone. This is viewed more negatively than any other lifestyle and yet women do live with each other, often in preference to any other way of life. Women raise children together, often with great success, but the fear of social censure and of legal and social work intervention may necessitate careful presentation, or denial of these living arrangements (Rights of Women, 1984; Rights of Women Lesbian Custody Group, 1986; Hanscombe and Forster, 1982).

7. The increasing number of women who live without men

because women live longer than men. In the age group 75–84, six out of ten are women and of those aged 85 and older seven out of ten are women (*cf* Walker, 1987).

Many women live alone at the end of their lives. Yet living alone is something that is supposed to happen only at the end of one's life and then inadvertently. Living alone is believed to be a poor second to marriage. One of Sophie Tucker's songs, '*I'm Living Alone and I Like It,*' expresses a deviant point of view. Women are not supposed to like it, but we all know of exceptions. For example, one of us had a grandmother who never looked back once her husband died. A much more fulfilling life of paid employment and social independence opened up for her.

Although they constitute a very small proportion statistically, a number of women never marry. Unmarried women enjoy better mental health than those who do, but they may be expected to give up employment to look after ageing parents or other relations (Bernard, 1972; Wright, 1983). Living alone does not mean that women are free from domestic responsibilities towards others.

Irrespective of the actual lives of women, there are commonly accepted organising principles governing our views about the happiness and social correctness of women's lives. These are:

1. whether or not women are living with men
2. whether or not women have children and
3. whether or not woman take appropriate responsibilities for dependent relatives.

Consciously to choose not to live with men, not to have children and not to care for dependent relatives, are seen as deviant behaviours. These deviances are ranked in order of importance. Not to live with men is the greatest deviance, followed by not having children, while the least deviant is not caring for dependent relatives. An inability to achieve either marriage or children, when these are seen to be desired and sought by the woman, is more likely to result in sympathy from family, friends, neighbours and society generally. Conscious deviance, however, can result in censure and efforts to recall the woman to the 'correct' way of life. As many young women know, the lack of a boyfriend or marriage plans can lead to expressions of repeated concern and even efforts to effect introductions and direct questioning of intentions.

These ideological responses to and demands on women can be experienced as devastatingly oppressive and restrictive. But even for women who want nothing more than to meet these demands, the struggle to achieve and maintain a 'socially correct life' is made particularly difficult by the social context in which many women, and especially social workers' clients, live. Access to social resources is often limited for women by this context.

These life patterns create and are based on women's financial dependency on men and the state. This is why participants on the Social Service Needs of Women courses reported that financial needs and housing issues were the problems most often brought to social workers by women. The economic context in which our women clients live is that of poverty which is interlinked with inadequate housing and poor health. This triangle of conditions forms the backdrop of women's lives whether clients of social services, of probation, or of voluntary agencies.

What is poverty?

> Women are 50 per cent of the global population
> Women are one-third of the paid labour force
> Women work two thirds of all working hours
> Women receive one-tenth of the world's income
> Women own less than 1 per cent of the world's property

Before we explore the poverty women live with and amidst, we must consider what we mean by poverty. The way we conceive of poverty will influence not only how we attempt to measure and alleviate it, but also its very nature and the way we think it is experienced. Definitions of poverty have varied over time and are hotly debated today. Rowntree in the late nineteenth century took as his base what was required to ensure 'merely physical efficiency'; that which was necessary for human survival. Adequate clothing for a young woman was 'one pair of boots, two aprons, one second hand dress, one skirt made from an old dress, a third of the cost of a new hat, a third of the cost of a shawl, and a jacket, two pairs of stockings, a few unspecified underclothes, one pair of stays and one pair of old boots worn as slippers' (Townsend, 1979, p. 50).

Today poverty is viewed in relation to a generally accepted standard of living that goes beyond basic physical needs and material well-being. When assessing poverty we must also include our social well-being because our needs are socially constructed and are not solely physical and material. People in poverty are those 'deprived of the conditions of life which ordinarily define membership of society' (Townsend, 1979, p. 915). So people must have enough income and command over resources which enable them to participate in the life of the community. What is hotly debated is which conditions should be measured and what constitutes a minimum standard of living.

Townsend's relative deprivation definition of poverty looked at food, clothing, utilities, employment, health, schooling, neighbourhood, leisure and social life. The study considered the quality of life as well as physical survival and income. Using these indicators, Townsend concluded that 35 per cent of the population in the 1960s was living in poverty, but this increased to 50 per cent when the number of people in poverty for any part of the year was added. Using the Government's own statistics the number of people living in poverty has increased during the 1970s and 1980s. Between 1979 and 1983 there was a 47 per cent increase in the number of people and a 72 per cent increase in the number of children living on or below the level of supplementary benefit (Child Poverty Action Group, 1987).

Sources of poverty

To speak of poverty is to speak of inequality (Scott, 1984, Glendinning & Millar 1987). The sources of inequality are usually defined in terms of class, gender and race. These factors interact in the lives of people. Poverty is widely associated with social class, but in recent years greater attention is being given to examining the disadvantages gender and race bring.

The phrase 'feminisation of poverty' describes women's position so that whether employed or unemployed, the majority of women cannot get out of poverty or escape the danger of being catapulted into it. Many women are dependent on the income of the man they live with for their class status, and lose their position and their lifestyle when their relationship ends. Women in employment are often kept poor because of their low wages and the number of children and adults who are dependent on them. The growing number of one-parent families in the UK, which are mostly headed by women, are especially vulnerable to poverty. In the US families headed by women account for 15 per cent of all families, but nearly half of all poor families (Scott, 1984).

Race, too, is a significant source of inequality and poverty (Cook and Watt, 1987). A Department of the Environment survey on racial disadvantages looked at unemployment, overcrowding, households lacking exclusive use of amenities, one-parent households, pensioners living alone and ethnic origin in order to develop relevant indicators (1983). These were used, for example, to examine the circumstances of black people both before and after the uprising of 1985 in the areas of Birmingham where the majority of black people live: Handsworth, Soho, and Lozell. Using the Department of Environment's indicators 70 per cent of Lozell is 'extremely deprived' as compared with 49 per cent of Birmingham's inner city (Report of the Review Panel, 1986, p. 20). The authors point out that in these areas many of the same afflictions are shared by poor whites: 'What divides black and white is racism' (p. 13). Whether we are looking at housing, environment or day care for the under fives, it is clear that, though not their exclusive preserve, ethnic minorities experience poverty and its accompanying conditions in greater degrees than the white population (DHSS, 1984; Home Affairs Select Committee, 1981). There is a danger that the impact of environmental poverty and racism is forgotten in the social work concentration on individuals and 'fit' or 'good' mothers. Understanding the wider meaning of poverty is crucial and it is to this that we now turn.

The dimensions of poverty

Poverty affects all aspects of life. It is about not having access to basic material goods and services. But it is also about living in a run-down environment with no resources, and with no space to dream. It is about how these things compound and interact with one another. For women this interaction of factors is pervasive because the home is their industrial workplace (Frankenburg, 1966). Women labour in the home, often in substandard conditions and constantly have to deal with the problem of 'doing without'.

The experience of poverty has a profound effect on women's lives and and on their children and the adults for whom they care, including the quality of their lives. In a conversation about race and class as interacting oppressions, Beverly Smith comments, 'When I think of poverty, I think of constant physical and material oppression. You know, you aren't poor one day and well-to-do the next. If you're poor it's a constant thing, everyday, everyday. In some ways it's almost more constant than race because, say you're middle class and you're a black person who is of course subject to racism, you don't necessarily experience it every single day in the same intensity, or to the same degree' (Smith and Smith, 1981, p. 115).

So being poor is not simply about doing without things. It is also about experiencing poor health, isolation, stress, stigma and exclusion, and feeling powerless. Women are especially vulnerable to all these dimensions of poverty and more. Poverty increases vulnerability to reception into care (National Council for One-Parent Families, 1983). Environment as well as income is a significant factor affecting decisions to take children into care. Holman found that in addition to low income, poor housing and geographical location were affecting child care decisions (1980). The vulnerability of black children to reception into care is now recognised. Racism and the factors identified by Holman locates the statistics on black children in care in a broader context. This improves our understanding of why black children are more likely to be taken into care and enables a question to be raised about the appropriateness of this remedy.

Living in poverty demands greater physical and psychological effort and stamina from women who take on family based caring responsibilities. By not interpreting the unpaid work women do as work, it is possible to ignore the skills and needs of women in a way that is not possible in paid work. The connection between the task expected of the worker and the economic means for carrying it out is obscured for all but the woman herself. She stands alone with this knowledge and her difficult-to-impossible work environment. Shifting the burden onto individual women in this way creates physical, mental and emotional stress for women as workers.

The stress in the struggle to survive poverty is illustrated well by one task expected of women – making and maintaining connections with numerous different agencies. The lack of material resources for day-to-day living means that the poor are often in continuous contact with the DHSS, the Gas and Electricity Boards, and housing departments. These departments are separate entities. But the effects of clients having to decide whether to use money for heating or for food has a direct impact on their housing conditions – housing stock can deteriorate because of damp – and health. These in turn will have an effect on the demands made on health and social services.

Poverty may also bring with it educational problems for children. Poverty often compounds educational disadvantages for black children, which is further complicated by racism. Racism is experienced as 'channelling and educating Black people into particular jobs, picking on Afro-Caribbean children and the new generation of Asian children as "troublemakers", and treating them as sub-human. Teachers are seen mainly as ones who don't expect Black people to get jobs or be able to learn' (Report of the Review Panel, 1986, p. 39). This problem was identified in the early 1960s, but little progress has been made in the acceptance of Afro-Caribbean and Asian cultures and languages. Racism means that black mothers must intervene and negotiate on behalf of their children in the education system. While white mothers, and in particular working-class mothers, also undertake these tasks, black mothers have the additional dimension of racism to contend with.

It is women who negotiate with these various bodies; just, as it is women who present themselves at social services with their families' problems. Women undertake these negotiations even when they are employed or when the men with whom they live are unemployed. Carrying responsibility for making and maintaining connections with agencies – what we in social work call liaison work – is often accepted without question as the woman's job; it is an integral component of her role as carer. Social workers are well aware that this work is time-consuming even with access to telephones and cars. Clients often are without these resources.

Housing

Poor, inadequate housing and homelessness are the consequences of poverty. Poor quality council and private rented housing is occupied by the most disadvantaged women, men and children in our society. To be poor is to have insufficient money to buy or rent spacious, good quality housing in 'good' neighbourhoods, but additionally, the quality of housing, particularly council housing, varies regionally. Some areas have sufficient housing stock, but a substantial proportion will be in bad condition and it is in this type of housing that the poorest live. Where there is sufficient housing stock, there may not be employment opportunities. Other areas, particularly London and the surrounding districts, offer better employment prospects, but have a major housing deficit.

Black people often live in conditions significantly worse than the general population. Black tenants of council housing are likely to live in flats rather than in houses; to be housed in flats furthest away from the ground; and if they live in houses they are likely to be in the poorest condition. (Brown, 1984; BASW, 1982). There is evidence that in some local authorities black people are discriminated against in the allocation of council houses and flats. They suffer harassment on estates from neighbours. (Report of the Review Panel, 1986; Commission for Racial Equality, 1984). Although some councils are taking steps to change this situation, it can mean that black families are concentrated on certain estates and these can be in worse condition than many of the other properties owned by the local authority.

The problem of poor housing for women is especially pronounced because housing policy is predicated upon families with male breadwinners. This puts pressure on women to become and remain attached to male bread-winners. Women's housing prospects are closely tied to their family status and ideals of domesticity and family life (Pascall, 1986). Women without men have limited access to owner occupation because of their low incomes and attitudes towards the commitment and capacity of women to remain in the labour market. Women, and poor women especially, are heavily reliant on public sector housing policies and these are powerful conditioning factors in their lives.

The increase in marriage breakdowns means that many women are faced with the issue of finding independent access to housing. Marital breakup can lead to poverty. Women can get caught in a downward spiral of high mortgage payments, arrears and ultimately homelessness. These housing stresses are especially severe for women forced out of their homes by violence. The growth of Women's Aid with its network of refuges highlights the connections between poverty, housing and health.

The economic and family relationships on which housing finance and allocation are based marginalise one-parent families. As the Finer Report commented: 'housing problems closely rival money problems as a cause of hardship and stress to one-parent families' (DHSS, 1974, p. 357). The housing tenure of single parents is a clear indication of their disadvantage and difference from other families. As the Housing Services Advisory Group points out, 'They are far less likely to be owner-occupiers, are more dependent on local authority housing and are particularly concentrated in private furnished accommodation' (Housing Services Advisory Group, 1978, p. 4). The private sector contains the worst of all housing conditions and is the most expensive. Thus one-parent families often live in poor and insecure accommodation at high costs.

In the public sector the Finer Report showed that unmarried mothers face discrimination from some local authorities and received the worst quality housing in the worst areas (DHSS, 1974). Yet it remains the main recourse for those women who have a high risk of being homeless. Where councils are unable to provide established housing, women often find themselves in temporary accommodation. There is a danger that the numerous young women with dependent children in bed and breakfast accommodation in inner city areas will be forgotten, or by sleight of hand will be excluded from our thinking about housing problems. Although their living conditions are slightly better than the night shelters in which increasing numbers of people are sleeping, the stress on women and their children who may remain in unsuitable, temporary accommodation, often for months, is enormous (McKechnie and Wilson, 1986).

The single homeless woman suffers not only from the shortage of accommodation which confronts the single homeless, but also from services which incompletely recognise her gender-related needs. While the Women's National Commission report of 1981 considered that single homeless women found their situation less stressful than did men, in our experience this opinion often is not shared by the women themselves or those working with them. Indeed the problem tends to be hidden, but still severe. Single women are not defined as in 'priority need' according to the Housing (Homeless Persons) Act 1980. Therefore they are not only invisible in local authority homelessness statistics, but are not catered for by this sector.

The traditional image of homeless single people tends to be male, the most extreme version being that of the male tramp under the arches. Because fewer women are to be seen sleeping rough, there is an assumption that fewer women than men become homeless. Rarely do we stop to question this or to find out if there are really fewer homeless women around or if women adopt different solutions to their housing problems or homelessness (Austerberry and Watson, 1983, p. 1).

Gillian Pascall has suggested what is important to understand is 'the way deprivation relates to women, to women's position in public, and private life, and to the state's defence of a certain kind of family structure' (Pascall, 1985, p. 149).

Health

The triangle of poverty and substandard housing is completed by poor health. This was a major concern of the social workers on the Social Service Needs of Women courses. Although obviously a key focus for hospital-based workers, poor health also was a prominent feature in the discussions of field and day centre workers. Their concerns ranged from the debilitating effects of parenting physically-handicapped children to drug and alcohol abuse. Nearly everyone used the term 'depression' to describe health problems of women clients.

In general both probation officers and area team workers related women's health problems to their role as carers of men, children and dependent adults in a context of poverty. Medical social workers, in particular, noted the guilt experienced by women who were too ill or handicapped to go on with the cleaning, cooking and caring for their families. Some commented that this was seen as a personal and gendered failure for women, one which made them feel 'unfeminine'.

These findings are very much in line with the literature on women's health. While there has been little work on the general health of women who are abused by men in the home, the Welsh Women's Aid study of the employment position of women who went through their refuges found that 51 per cent of the interviewed women reported health problems and 19 per cent described themselves as having nervous disorders (1980). In a study of mothers and daughters, both the older and younger generation of women were found to have a conception of normal health described by the researchers as 'low', and the older women had developed a high tolerance for pain and discomfort (Blaxter & Patterson, 1982, p. 185). The level of income on which many clients have to manage is too low to meet the health needs of the woman and her family. (Graham, 1984).

The picture is very different from that painted in the Fowler Review where the main problem is seen as the inability to budget rather than the inadequacy of the benefits levels (DHSS, 1985). Thus it is largely women whom the Fowler Review criticises for an inability to budget and holds responsible for the harm this does to others. Yet there is growing evidence that women reduce their personal consumption to aid the collective consumption of their family. In other words they are the first to feel the effects of any economies. Such strategies are very apparent amongst unemployed women (Callender, 1987a). Cutting back on food and heating for the entire family are the most amenable to further economies. Women are forced to make choices between health keeping and housekeeping (Graham, 1987). The consequences of budget deficits for health are particularly marked for the very young and the very old, i.e. those for whom women care.

The effect of these coping strategies on women's health is both hidden and unknown. There is now a considerable literature on the effects of unemployment on men's health (Hill, 1977; Colledge, 1981; Smith, 1987), while much less attention is paid to how unemployment affects women's health. The unemployment of a husband or cohabitee influences not only the man's health but also that of the woman and the children with whom he lives (Graham, 1984, p. 76). Women also often give up a job or give up looking for one, when a man becomes unemployed because of the effect her employment has on the family's supplementary benefits. She is then left to cope on a dramatically reduced income, with an increased likelihood of illness among her children and her own personal reactions to unemployment as well as those of the man with whom she is living.

Transport

Access to transport is another important resource which tends to get ignored when examining dimensions of inequality and poverty. Car ownership is directly related to social class and gender (LeGrand, 1982). In social class I 85 per cent of households have a car compared to 28 per cent in social class V. Only about one quarter of all women have a driving licence compared to over two-thirds of men. When a car is available men usually have priority use of it; women have to walk or rely on public transport. Indeed three-quarters of all bus passengers are women. However, this transport is rarely designed for women. Often there is nowhere to put shopping or a push chair and this is especially the case with the new mini-buses recently introduced since the de-regulation of bus services.

With the reduction in bus servives and increases in fares in recent years, options for women to get out of the home and off the estates or out of the areas in which they live are diminishing. As women are mainly responsible for liaising with agencies the decrease in services means they have to struggle harder to reach the resources necessary for their families' well-being, such as doctors, health centres, social security offices, food and other shops and play facilities. Women in rural areas and on large housing estates are particularly adversely affected. These problems of access show how far we are from realising the principle of organising key services within 'pram pushing distance' (Richards, 1987). Planners rarely consider the needs of women when locating facilities and services.

Some counties limit the transport provided by social services to day centres within a given radius from the town centre. The elderly, the mentally handicapped and mentally ill adults are the most isolated of all from resources unless transport can be arranged. The carer, too, does not get a break when decisions are based on geographical criteria and not on the need of either the client or the carer.

Access to transport is one means of increasing personal safety for women. During the five year period when the mass murderer of women, the so-called 'Ripper', roamed the North of England, women showed their understanding of transport as a means of improving their safety. Women who usually walked acquired bicycles, those who usually cycled moved onto buses and so on. Black women face the same dangers as white women and in addition, the likelihood of more frequent racial and sexual attacks.

The extensive literature on poverty and its impact rarely specifically examines the poverty of women (Glendinning and Millar, 1987). Poverty for women entails not only a low income and struggles from day to day to make ends meet in poor physical surroundings, but it also contributes to a worsening of mental and physical health along with a major reduction in options and opportunities generally. However women are not the passive victims of poverty. As we have seen they use their skills to manage and overcome it. They look to whatever resources are available to them in this struggle. One of these resources is employment.

Questions

1. Think of the women with whom you have worked or know. How is poverty affecting their lives?
2. Are the black or ethnic minority families with whom you work or know financially worse off than the white families? If they are what effect is this having on the lives of Afro-Caribbean, Asian, and other ethnic minority women?
3. Are agencies more responsive to the needs of one-parent families headed by men than by women? What factors do you think influence this outcome?
4. What are the major housing issues for the women with whom you work? Are some women more adversely affected than others? How would you explain these differences?

5. Do you think women clients' physical and mental health problems are related to their role as carers of men, children and dependent adults in a context of poverty? If not, what other factors are particularly relevant?

3

Women and the Labour Market: A Contradiction for Social Work

with Claire Callender

Over the years in teaching on social work courses, we have observed women using social work training as a way out of unemployment and/or poverty for themselves and their families. Some of the women on the Social Service Needs of Women courses expressed guilt about the better working conditions they experienced in comparison with women clients. We see the feelings of guilt as a recognition of commonalities between women social workers and clients. However, these commonalities cannot be expressed easily because of the way the social work task is understood and carried out in their social work agencies. This is another example of institutionalised sexism where women social workers are called upon to reinforce women's responsibilities as wives, mothers and carers, and to ignore the poverty and employment issues facing women clients.

Being in employment is an important factor in keeping families out of poverty. Of unemployed one-parent families, 87 per cent live below the poverty line as opposed to 37 per cent of lone parents who are in employment (Popay *et al.*, 1982). One-parent families are particularly vulnerable to poverty because they do not have the option of combining two wages to maintain living standards as do 50 per cent of two-parent families. This explains why one-third of low income families with children are one-parent families.

Women's lack of educational opportunities and training, low pay and the shortage of day care facilities are factors in keeping women dependent on benefits. Of one-parent families headed by men 70 per cent have earnings as their main source of income in contrast with 44.6 per cent headed by women (Popay *et al.*, 1982). Greater earning power enable men to purchase day care and other forms of help such as housekeepers (DHSS, 1974), and social services are more responsive to requests for assistance from one-parent families headed by men even though their resources are greater than those headed by women.

Women in two-parent families are not untouched by poverty. Most clients of social workers are working-class and a substantial proportion are manual workers who are more vulnerable to unemployment than any other occupational group as are the women who live with and depend on the income of male manual workers. A small porportion of men have earnings which barely exceed what they would receive on supplementary benefit. Low pay means two incomes become necessary to escape poverty, or that very long hours of overtime have to be worked to make ends meet.

Young families are more likely to be affected by unemployment because of the higher proportion of unemployed people in the under-25 age group. The families of the long-term unemployed have more children; (117 per 100 households) than those where one or more parents are employed (96 children per 100 households) (Hughes, 1985).

Women's own unemployment is a direct source of poverty forcing women to rely on benefits. It also has implications for the woman's future employment prospects. Given the decline in the number of full-time jobs for women a number are forced into part-time work, others into less skilled and lower paid full-time work (Coyle, 1984; Callender, 1987a; 1987b). We have already seen that women, young people and men who are black are more vulnerable to low pay and unemployment than the white population so that the experience of poverty is unevenly distributed between black and white people. Another variable that has to be born in mind is in the uneven distribution of unemployment throughout the UK. The West Midlands, the North of

England, Scotland, Wales and Northern Ireland are the most affected (Hughes 1985). Unemployment generates adverse social conditions; it affects not only conditions within the home but the environment itself. De-industrialisation leaves empty factories, mills and mines as part of the landscape in which people live.

Responsibility for managing on very low incomes whether caused by unemployment, low pay, living on benefits or unequal sharing of household resources falls on women. How income is shared within the home needs more attention from social workers as even when in employment and when earnings are good, men may fail to provide financial support to the women and children with whom they live or they may do so only erratically or at a level below the poverty line (see Chapter 5). Women clients can be better off when their husbands are in prison or when they leave and women can claim social security in their own right (Brannen and Wilson, 1987).

The way women's economic subordination is institutionalised makes women's poverty difficult to raise as an issue in social work. The economically dependent woman is the ideal client. She is available as the carer of dependent children and adults in the family and a vital resource for community care, which is usually located in the privacy of the home. Her employment outside the home reduces her availability within it even though her employment may keep the family out of poverty or seriously reduce it. This is a major reason why this chapter was the most difficult to integrate into a book on social work practice. Another is the way the public-private division of society is conceptualised in social theory. Employment is largely presented as the antithesis of home based life both for men and women. This falsifies the integration of home and paid employment, particularly for women, thus distorting the role of paid employment in women's experience of life and personal identity.

Women and employment

Work tends to be seen as paid, full-time, continuous and outside the home. However, this model of work is male-dominated and does not reflect the reality of most women's experiences. Much of women's work is invisible and unrecorded in the national income. Moreover, because women's work does not 'fit' this model, it is marginalised (Callender, 1985).

A radical change in lifestyles and life patterns has resulted from the increased number of women in paid work. This number rose from 6.5 million in 1951 to 9.2 million in 1981 and is expected to rise to 9.6 million by 1990 (Beechey, 1985). By contrast, the number of men in the labour force decreased from 13.5 million in 1951 to 12.9 million in 1981. Paid employment for women is no longer a luxury women can choose whether or not to pursue. For the vast majority it is a necessity as families can no longer survive on one pay packet. It is estimated that three times as many families would be in poverty if the wife was not employed (Hamill, 1978) and 60 per cent of wives contribute to the family budget (DHSS, 1985). Paid employment is a normal part of women's lives; over half were economically active in 1985 compared to three-quarters of men. For women of West Indian origin this figure rises to over two-thirds (*Labour Force Survey*, 1985).

Which women are employed?

The growth in female employment is primarily amongst married women and especially those with young children. In 1951 only one in five married women were employed compared to one in two now (Oakley, 1981). About a half of married women with children under 16 now work and two-thirds with children over school age. The age of a woman's youngest child, especially if it is under 5, will determine whether she is employed, if her job is full- or part-time and the type of work she undertakes. Marriage is no longer a crucial determinant of women's participation in the labour market.

Women are spending an increasing proportion of their lives in paid work, although few adopt the typical male pattern of continuous employment. Most women work full-time until the birth of their first child. In the past these women would have returned to employment once their children had grown up. Women are now returning to employment more quickly after childbirth and an increasing number are returning to employment between births, mostly to part-time jobs.

Where do women work?

The labour market is segregated by sex and women are highly concentrated in certain sectors of the economy, in particular the service sector. This is known as horizontal segregation. In 1985 over three-quarters of women employees were concentrated in only four occupations: clerical; catering, cleaning, hairdressing and other personal services; professional and related in education, welfare and health; and selling (*Labour Force Survey*, 1985). This occupational distribution applies to both black and white women. However, white women are especially concentrated in clerical occupations; 30 per cent compared to 23 per cent of black women. Black women are more numerous in processing and assembling occupations (*Labour Force Survey*, 1985). Over the years women's segregated position in the labour force has become even more entrenched (Hakim, 1979). Janet Holland came to the conclusion that 'for women occupational choice is a misnomer, it does not exist' (1980, p. 15).

   Within occupations women are concentrated in the bottom grades and this is known as vertical segregation. Although more women are entering the professions, they do not reach higher positions in proportion to their numbers. The status of the job holder seems to correlate directly with the sex of the job holder. Social work demonstrates this pattern as the higher up the occupational ladder the fewer the number of women. Women are found disproportionately in the lower professional grades even though they are in the majority in social services (Popplestone, 1980, 1981; Howe, 1986). The numerical dominance of women is further emphasised if all workers in social services departments are included; that is, clerical and secretarial staff, domestics, care assistants, social work assistants. Men begin to predominate in social work, as in other occupations, at the level of management (see Chapter 7). Women social workers share with their clients these patterns of working with men.

There are some significant differences in the occupational concentration of full-time and part-time women workers. In 1984 the distribution of women full-time workers was: 42 per cent clerical, 19 per cent professional in education, welfare and health, 9 per cent catering and cleaning, etc., 6 per cent selling. The equivalent proportions for part-time women workers was 22 per cent, 17 per cent, 40 per cent, 12 per cent (*New Earnings Survey*, 1984). The sorts of jobs open to women wanting part-time work are rather different to those available to women who can work full-time.

Part-time workers

One of the most dramatic changes in the structure of the labour market generally and for women in particular, is the increase in part-time jobs. This rise accounts for nearly *all* the increase in women's employment since the 1950s and part-time work is the only area where the numbers of employees is continuing to rise despite the recession. Women account for 89 per cent of all part-time workers (*Labour Force Survey*, 1985), and 70 per cent of employed women with dependent children work part-time (Equal Opportunities Commission, 1985, p. 26). So the presence of children and domestic responsibilities have a strong influence on the number of hours women can do paid work. It has been suggested that part-time jobs are being constructed specifically as jobs for married women (Beechey and Perkins 1987). But women in one-parent families are less likely than married women to work part-time and more likely to work full-time.

The service sector employs 90 per cent of part-time workers, especially in less 'skilled' and lower paid jobs like cleaning, clerical work, waitressing and in the lower level jobs in the welfare state. Virtually all women's manual work in health, education and the social services is organised on a part-time basis, as is most caring work done by unqualified women in hospitals and residential establishments (Beechey, 1985).

Although part-time employment offers women a practical way to resolve tensions between domestic responsibilities and waged work there are distinct disadvantages to this employment. Most jobs are in the lower paid sectors of the economy. Part-time workers often have limited entitlement to fringe benefits, good employment conditions, such as sick pay, holidays, promotion and training opportunities. For example, in 1984 three-fifths of part-time workers earned too little to pay National Insurance contributions and so were ineligible for contributory social security benefits, such as unemployment benefit or sick pay or income-related pensions. Usually part-time workers are poorly unionised and less protected under the employment protection legislation. This means they are cheap and easy to dismiss which makes them attractive to employers.

Pay

In Britain, despite equal pay legislation, the gap between men and women's pay remains considerable (Low Pay Unit, 1987). Based on an hourly rate, for every £100 an average man earns, the average women earns only £73.5 (Department of Employment, 1984). The result of these disparities is the large number of women who are low paid. Nearly six million of all the low paid, 67 per cent, are women and nearly four million, 43 per cent, are part-time workers (Low Pay Unit, 1987). Recent changes in legislation affecting Wages Councils, and the Conservative Government's attempts to deregulate the labour market so that workers do not 'price themselves out of jobs', mean that the situation is likely to get worse. Thus an increasing number of women will earn their poverty.

Homeworkers are often singled out as one of *the* most exploited groups of workers, working for extremely low rates of pay for long hours without employment protection, decent work conditions and social security rights. Home-work is done almost exclusively by women and, in particular, by black and ethnic minority women (Allen and Wolkowitz, 1987) We have insufficient knowledge about homeworkers nationally, but in 1981 homeworkers were estimated to number at least 229 800, and a third earned less than £10 per week, while three-quarters earned less than £40 per week (Allen and Wolkowitz, 1987; Hakim, 1987).

Women's low pay is primarily attributable to where they work, the type of work they do and sex bias in skill definitions and evaluations. Women are employed in the lowest paying sectors of the economy. Their low pay is also affected by their discontinuous employment patterns. On returning to employment after a break in their service, women often experience downward occupational mobility. They enter poorly paid part-time jobs for which they are over qualified (Dex, 1987). Adherence to the notion of a family wage and a sole male breadwinner by both employers and trade unionists is used as justification for low wages and the perpetuation of the myth that women only work for pin money.

Both white and black women earn less than white or black men. In the USA it is estimated that white women earn 60 per cent of white men's wages and black women earn 80 per cent of black men's wages (Solomon, 1987). In the UK we do not have the information to compare white and black women's average wages, but in the USA the rank order from greater to lesser earnings is white men, black men, white women, black women. Black single mothers both in the labour force and outside of it have less income than white mothers in a similar situation (Burden and Gottleib, 1987, p. 32). Observation suggests that the same pattern of inequality prevails in Britain.

Casualisation and unemployment

The increasing concentration of women in low paid, unskilled and part-time employment working under poor working conditions points to the casualisation of women's work.

Their jobs are often very insecure and they can be easily and cheaply dismissed. There is considerable debate on the extent to which women or certain groups of women workers are particularly susceptible to unemployment in comparison to men (Callender, 1985).

Official statistics suggest that women make up one-third of the total unemployed and that women's unemployment has risen at a much faster rate than men's. Figures based upon those claiming social security benefits show that between 1979 and 1986 male unemployment rose by 130 per cent while female unemployment increased by 162 per cent (Child Poverty Action Group, 1987). However, these figures need to be treated with caution. Women's unemployment may be 1 million to 1.25 million greater than the monthly Department of Employment statistics suggest (Callender, 1987b) because the figure is based only on those claiming social security benefits, and many women do not register.

There are several explanations for this. First those who have paid the married women's stamp are not eligible for unemployment benefit. Secondly, many women are denied access to benefits because they are not deemed 'available for work'. For instance, women with dependent children are required to prove that they have made day care arrangements which can take effect immediately should a job be offered in order to be eligible for unemployment benefit and to register. These are major disincentives which serve to reinforce informal means of finding jobs rather than using the Government's job centres (Coyle, 1984; Callender, 1987a, 1987b). Restrictions on eligibility for benefits and registration for women means that they do not have access to certain jobs, such as those offered through the Government's Community Programme. The Equal Opportunities Commission attempt to challenge this practice as sex discrimination was unsuccessful.

The data available on the differential rates of unemployment between white and black women is limited, but black women are nearly twice as likely as white women to be unemployed. In all age groups unemployment is higher among black women than white women. However, the unemployment rates between ethnic minority groups vary considerably by age (*Labour Force Survey*, 1985). Unemployment remains higher for black women than white women with the same broad level of education (Department of Employment, 1987).

Although it is often invisible, women's unemployment cannot be ignored or marginalised. We cannot assume that unemployed women will be absorbed into the home or that they will not experience financial and psychological hardship (Callender, 1987a, 1987b). Initially women, like men, may treat redundancy as a temporary feature of their lives, thinking of it as a holiday and focusing their attention on the home (Levie, Gregory and Lorentzen, 1984). This can be agreeable to men who benefit from the increased time, but still have women to do the housework, to cook, and to be their companions. Women do not slip neatly back into the domestic and caring roles when they lose their paid work and housework cannot compensate for paid employment. Both Angela Coyle's and Claire Callender's research show that, as with men, the impact varies with the circumstances of the woman; for example, whether or not she is the sole or primary economic provider, or whether or not she is intending to have a child (Coyle, 1984; Callender, 1987b). Many women have to take jobs which are temporary, less well paid, less skilled, and part-time, if they can find employment at all. In regions of high unemployment it is not unusual to find both husband and wife without paid employment.

Women's vulnerability in the labour market is given ideological legitimation by the economic recession and monetarist philosophy. There is a revival of ideas which suggest that women do not have a right to paid employment and their place is in the home caring for the family. Women's employment opportunities and their access to employment are restricted, it becomes more difficult to combine their 'dual role', and there is disenfranchisement of women's rights at work. As a result women may accept the 'queueing principle' (Martin and Wallace, 1984). In times of high unemployment certain social groups, in particular men, are felt to have a greater claim to paid employment (Callender, 1987b).

One of the effects of the recession has been to produce new patterns of employment and an increase in labour market flexibility. Employees can be divided into two groups: full-time 'permanent' employees and other 'flexible' workers. By the mid-1980s the labour force was divided into two-thirds 'permanent' and one-third 'flexible'. A quarter of all men in work, but over a half of all women (5 million plus), are now in the 'flexible' sector (Hakim, 1987). The position of women workers reflects wider changes in the restructuring of the economy and social welfare. This is no compensation for women who must support themselves or for women who must support their families, nor does it necessarily reduce the working day for women.

Whether in full-time or in part-time employment or not, there is a continuing disparity between the length of the working day for women in comparision with men. Women work on average 12–15 hours a day as opposed to 9 hours for men. Men spend less than one hour a day in domestic work and tend to overestimate the amount they do according to their wives' reports (*Social Trends*, 1986, p. 36). Balancing paid employment and domestic work involves pressures. For example, one study found that stress on women in factory work arose less from the job itself than from all the shopping they had to do before going home and their work once there (Shimmin *et al.*, 1981).

Changes in training are needed for social workers to begin to take on board the reality of women's experiences of both employment *and* unemployment. Social workers must consider the consequences and pains of unemployment for women just as they do for men. It is only then that the strenuous living conditions of women can be appreciated, and assessments of and plans made for the three most common demands made on women. These are caring for children, dependent adults, and maintaining relationships with men, along with the impact these have on the identity and self esteem of women.

Questions

1. Why do you think social work literature and practice is so indifferent to women's employment?
2. Do you agree that it is the nature of the work expected of social workers that makes it so difficult to perceive commonalities in the employment situations of women social workers and clients?
3. What patterns of employment can you observe amongst the women with whom you work? Do women work continuously? When do women go part-time? When do women give up paid work altogether?
4. How is unemployment affecting the women with whom you work? Do women tend to give up their jobs when their husbands or cohabitees become unemployed? Is redundancy a problem for the women with whom you work or know?
5. How is the unemployment of women affecting the triangle of poverty, poor housing and ill health amongst women with whom you work or know?

4

Women as Carers

Women have a career as carers (Finch and Groves, 1983; Ungerson, 1983, 1985). Women do not just look after children; a substantial number of women can expect to look after a dependent adult in their middle years and early old age (Hunt, 1970). Single women may also experience the role of carer. They are more likely than men to be called upon to look after either related children or other adults. Caring means work, even if it is carried out with love, and inevitably, when caring is combined with employment, 'the two are constantly in tension' (Finch and Groves, 1983, p. 7). The theme of caring is therefore a crucial one for women whether client or social worker.

Living with children

Most women have children; 80 per cent of women become mothers (General Household Survey Unit, 1978). Many social workers share the experience of being a mother with their women clients. Living with and caring for men, and producing, living with and caring for children are held to be basic to a woman's life. It is a state towards which many women strive but, as with living with men, the experiences we have of motherhood range from the very positive to the very negative (Boulton, 1983; Dally, 1982; Dalley, forthcoming; Dowrick and Grundberg, 1980; Arcana, 1983 and 1981; New and David, 1985; Rich, 1977; Riley, 1983).

Women carry the main burden of child care. This does not substantially alter even if the woman is employed, or if the man is unemployed, although there may be some reallocation of chores (Coyle, 1984; Graham, 1984). The old adage, 'Men work from sun to sun and women's work is never done', illustrates only one aspect of the work demands on women.

Child care is largely carried out in the socially isolating conditions of the one or two adult family household unit. The social isolation of women caring for children was a recurring theme raised by practitioners. The work of George Brown and Tirrel Harris into clinical depression of women with small children identified a lack of interaction at a deep personal level with another adult, i.e. social isolation, as one of its major indicators (1978). Clinical depression is, however, a greater problem for poorer women than for those whose social isolation has the possibility of being lessened by the possession of more material resources. The economic context of motherhood is thus significant and depression is one of the many adverse effects on mothers and children associated with poverty.

Adrienne Rich in *Of Woman Born* explores the context in which women must rear children (1977). In a deeply humane account of her own experience, she describes the conflicts between her desire and need for her three sons and the need to continue writing as a poet. This life-affirming account names the conditions of reproduction, the institution of motherhood itself, as the cause of her anguish. Rich identifies the elements of the institution of motherhood to be legal, economic, cultural and psychological. Alice Walker gives an account from a black woman's perspective that explores similar themes (1984).

To locate the problem of mothering solely in the social isolation of mothers, or in the separation of mothers from their children, neatly sidesteps a closer look at the complex interpenetration of the strands that make up the institution of motherhood as a whole. The problems become personalised. The woman's behaviour is seen as inappropriate. She is deemed unable to make and sustain relationships with children, men, family and neighbours.

Truly to understand the experience of mothers and mothering is to look beyond the mother–child relationship to the social forces and policies that shape and restrain its expression. Looked at in this way the experience of becoming a mother and caring for children is not inevitable, biologically dictated or a private matter unconnected to the rest of society, but the result of social organisation. The isolation is socially engineered, the result of policies and institutionalised practices some of which are located in social work agencies. That which is socially organised can be altered; the institution of motherhood is not fixed for all time in its present form.

'Fit mothering' and social work assessment

Child care was a priority for the practitioners on the courses. This reflects the concerns of social service departments (Parsloe and Stevenson, 1978) and the frequent reassertion of the importance of child care work, and of the child, client for example, the results of the enquiry into the death of Jasmine Beckford (Brent, 1985). The conditions in which children are being brought up, too often involve inadequate income with little or no access to resources that can relieve mothers of virtually total responsibility. Even when a man is part of the family women are seen, and see themselves, as being the person primarily responsible for child care.

Having a handicapped child adds to the usual requirements placed on women. Wilkin's research confirms that the additional burdens of caring for handicapped children fall mainly on the mothers (1979). In addition to providing day to day care, mothers are also mainly responsible for coping with out patient appointments, visits to and from hospital during periods of stay which are a regular feature of many handicapped children's lives (Baldwin and Glendenning, 1983).

The statutory responsibilities of departments are to a large extent centred on the care, protection and control of children and young people. A complex of laws (Short Report, 1984) require social workers to enforce minimum standards.

The assumption behind these laws, currently being reinforced by the Conservative Government's policies and by the ideology of the New Right, is that parenting is entirely a private, personal responsibility (Campbell, 1987; David 1983, 1985, 1986: Dworkin, 1983). Apart from specific aspects of health care and education, the acquisition of the social and economic conditions for 'good enough' parenting are assumed to be within the grasp and control of the parents themselves. But the way 'good enough' parenting is conceptualised minimises the recognition of the impact of the interaction of racism, sexism and social class on the social development of the child.

The spotlight falls on mothers as the responsible people and social work concurs with this judgement. For instance, in a review of child abuse cases where the child was living at home under supervision, the Social Service Inspectorate found a lack of information about male figures in the home (1986). This finding is a practical illustration of how the concept of the 'fit mother' operates within social work.

In most instances the idea of the 'fit mother' is more implicit than explicit. What is a fit mother? Each of us needs to be clear about the components, even though the idea is a developing and changing one. The cultural ideal contains the following components:

- providing adequate housing, warmth and food
- providing access to appropriate stimulation and learning opportunities
- providing suitable discipline, control and moral guidance
- reproducing of feminine and masculine identities in girls and boys
- having the characteristics of being responsive to children and able to suppress or delay gratification of one's own needs over long periods
- being able to provide uninterrupted caring and loving
- being heterosexual
- being able to establish and maintain over a long period a monogamous relationship with a man, preferably the biological father, who will provide economic support for the family.

For black women the concept of 'fit mother' has additional elements. First, it is eurocentric in minimising the importance of extended kin and neighbourhood to the family. Secondly, stereotypes can apply to the way black women are seen to provide care for their children. Afro-Caribbean women can be seen as either too harsh in their discipline or alternatively too lax, while Asian women can be seen as over-protective and providing so much caring that it becomes repressive (Bhavnani, 1987).

Motherhood, in our view, is becoming more tightly structured and the concept of 'fit mother' is becoming more tightly defined. Social workers, along with medical personnel, health visitors, social security officers and housing workers, monitor mothering from ante-natal care onwards. For example the concept of 'fit mother' is used by courts when assessing the offences committed by women. It is not the offence alone which is judged, but the appropriateness of the behaviour for a person who is, or may become, a rearer of the next generation. Initial light sentences are rapidly replaced by heavy penalties for the woman who re-offends (Carlen, 1983; Carlen *et al.*, 1985; Dobash and Dobash, 1986; Heidensohn, 1985; McLeod, 1982; Pattulo, 1983).

There is no corresponding 'fit father' role for social workers to use in their assessment and planning. Whether men contribute towards their families financially or emotionally or personally through making time available to be with children or not, they rarely lose their rights of access to and authority over children. Unlike motherhood, social workers are not expected, and do not expect, to monitor or improve expressions of fatherhood in the families they visit. This remains the case even though in families where the man is unemployed he may be encouraged to participate more in order to give him a role when his breadwinner function is lost. The consequence for social workers is to see the mother as the person on whom to concentrate. She is held responsible for breakdowns or failures in any area of a child's life and at any age; whether it occurs in the home, the neighbourhood, the school, in employment or during unemployment.

Day care and 'fit mothering'

Parenting, or mothering, is seen now as a difficult and, at times, arduous task. The view of the transmission of poverty through families, the so-called cycle of deprivation, led to calls in the 1960s for education for parenthood (Pringle, 1975, 1980). This has been met to some extent through school courses designed to prepare young people for this role. Day care is another means of relieving some of the pressures on mothers and teaching parenting skills to women who come into contact with social workers.

Family aides, family centres and day care are seen as a major means of relieving women of some of the burdens of looking after children in poverty and poor housing, including social isolation. State day-care resources are, however, minimal and are largely concentrated on a tiny minority of children defined as being at risk. In the past increasing state day-care provision was at least seen as desirable, even if too expensive for the state to provide (Mayall and Petrie, 1983). Now a few community nurseries go against a trend in policy to define day care as a private activity of mothers. These nursery places are benefiting children from ethnic minority groups and the white working class who tend to be under-represented in playgroups (DHSS, 1984). Black women must also cope with prejudice against themselves and their children in seeking and using daily minders. The range of available resources and their quality are lessened for black women (Mayall and Petrie, 1983). For the majority of women, however, day-care is provided through family, relatives, friends and neighbourhood play schemes. Women in employment also rely on these sources and, in addition, there is a large but unknown number of unregistered daily minders, estimated to account for about 62 per cent of all daily minding (Mayall and Petrie, 1983).

The ideology of 'fit mothering' requires that women provide all care for the very young child apart from exceptional occasions. Extensive well-conducted research demonstrating the capacity of young children to relate to more than one carer has not shifted this belief (Rutter, 1981; Schaeffer, 1977). Given the ideology of mother's responsibility it is not surprising that there is a marked lack of day-care for the under-threes, or that employment, but not unemployment, is seen as a problem for mothers. The reverse situation applies to fathers; unemployment is seen as a problem, but not employment.

Yet some women are thought to be good mothers even though or because they do not care continuously for their children. A system of au pairs, nannies and boarding school enables women with the economic means totally, or partially, to separate caring *about* their children from the tasks of caring *for* or tending them (Parker, 1981). Because of their class position the mothers who use this class-related system of care for their children are not viewed as inadequate by the state.

However, women who use state services, either because they recognise they cannot give day-to-day care or because they are assessed to have fallen below the minimum standard of care, are viewed extremely negatively. They also frequently view themselves in the same way. The resulting pattern of shared care with the state creates problems for both the child and the parent. The concept of fit mothering inhibits the development of approval for mothering that involves less than total day-to-day care for working- and lower-middle-class children.

Sharing care, even for parts of the day, raises the question of the children's needs and how these can be balanced against those of the mother. This formulation of the problem places on the woman the requirement to take, or demand, just enough space for herself, but not so much that it is deemed to be detrimental to the child. Similarly, social workers who consider it important for women to have space for themselves in order to be aware of and meet their own needs are faced with the question of balance. The definition of the needs of women and their children as conflictual is made within the institution of motherhood. 'Women have been made the main parties in that conflict, so that it can look as if women's freedom is *necessarily* threatening to children, while children's care *necessarily* requires women to set their personal sights low' (New and David, 1985, p.328).

One practical effect of this conflict in the lives of women is that in career terms, it is an advantage for a man to be married but a disadvantage for a woman. The question of balance in meeting children's needs, and as we shall see later, men's, does not arise for a single or a married man. A woman has to remain both single and childless to ensure that it does not arise for her.

Involuntary childlessness

Involuntary childlessness can happen biologically or socially, as motherhood is both a biological and a social experience. 'Involuntary childlessness in women is seen as a tragedy and voluntary childlessness at least an oddity' (New and David, 1985, p. 41). More women are having, and keeping, their babies than in the past. The decline in the number of babies for adoption over the last twenty years along with an intense pro-natalist ideology means that social workers are now meeting few women who are childless. They meet even fewer women who are voluntarily childless; in part because they are few in number and in part because social services is set up as family-based service.

The brief of the Seebohm Report (1968) was to advise on the organisation of social services as a family-based service. This objective is implicit in the Barclay Report where community care is described as family care (1982). Our social policy is structured on an assumption that people should live in biologically-based nuclear families. This assumption is so pervasive that it is largely unquestioned, and unquestionable. Observation suggests that both prescriptively and statistically the small family is the norm. In the public image, marriage, parenthood and the family are inextricably linked and prescribed avenues for those wishing to join 'the mature, the secure, the respectable and the adult' (Campbell, 1985).

Women who are without children, either from choice or because they cannot have a child biologically, were mentioned only once or twice on The Social Service Needs of

Women courses. Yet social workers, too, are involuntarily childless and live without children. This is one of the commonalities, and also diversities, identified by the course participants. Working with clients who were involuntarily childless raised for some social workers the question of whether or not they would find themselves in this position later on when attempting to conceive.

The main concerns that social workers on the courses expressed for women without children were for those who were separated from their children, either because these mothers are offenders and in prison, or were ill, addicted to drugs or alcohol, or had not met the standards of 'fit mothering'. Justifications for removing children from women can involve economic or social factors as well as negative assessments of mother–child interactions. For example, the risks of being physically removed from giving care to their children are high for women who are persistent offenders (Carlen, 1983). They are also high for lesbian mothers regardless of the standard of care being provided (Rights of Women, 1984; Rights of Women Lesbian Custody Group, 1986; Hanscombe and Forster, 1982).

Another example of the dominance of social factors is provided by children who are removed from mothers whose care is adequate if they are thought unable to control an abusing father or cohabitee. The unconscious assumption that women are responsible for all relationships within the household can mean punitive reactions against mothers once child sexual abuse is discovered, even when the mother reports the offence herself. Her initial disbelief that her husband could be abusing her daughter may be held against her, as may her fear of violence from him if she is unable to guarantee that she can single handedly evict the man should he come around again (Hanmer and Saunders, 1987).

The recent increase in attention given to the sexual abuse of children, where almost all offenders are men, raises in an acute form the need to examine ideological assumptions about 'fit mothering' and the lack of a corresponding 'fit fathering' concept. As long as mothers wish to care for their children, the threat and the actual removal of them is a powerful mode of social control and punishment. The assumption that caring is not men's work and abuse within the family is not 'real' crime, means that men are neither controlled nor punished. These problems will be explored further in the next chapter, but first we look at the remaining caring functions prescribed for women.

Caring for dependent adults

Like caring for children, caring for dependent adults is women's work. Care for the elderly was identified as a significant problem for women by the practitioners on our courses. This is partly the result of the low priority given to work with the elderly in area teams.

Cases involving the elderly are often given to social work assistants rather than qualified staff in field teams (Parsloe and Stevenson, 1978), and the elderly, mentally ill or handicapped may fall into the category 'unallocated', even though they are active cases (Goldberg and Warburton, 1979). Participants whose work was primarily with the elderly either in day centres, or in residential care, hospitals or area teams, quite rightly upbraided the rest of us who saw working with children as the major problem area in work with women. They also pointed out that a substantial proportion of the very old, and hence those in geriatric wards, day and residential care, were women. The needs of the black elderly may well be underestimated by social workers because it is assumed they will be looked after by an extended family. Cultural stereotyping in social work assessments can obscure the fact that black families are diverse. The black elderly person's support systems need as careful examination as those of the white elderly.

Many women have a cycle of caring beginning with caring for children, moving on to caring for elderly relatives and finally aged spouses (Rimmer, 1983, p. 142). Serial monogmy is a factor affecting the cycle of caring. Women in a first marriage tend to marry men who are similar in age or slightly older than themselves. Only a minority of husbands (2 per cent) are 10 years older than their wives. For second marriages, however, this figure rises to 23 per cent. In contrast, only 6 per cent of men have wives who are 10 years older than them (Rimmer, 1983). Thus at the end of their lives there are a number of women looking after the very old, a substantial proportion of whom will be their husbands. This pattern is not fully reciprocated, in part because 75 per cent of elderly men are married compared to 30 per cent of elderly women (Finch and Groves, 1983). The other women will be looking after relatives, friends, or neighbours at the end of their lives. As with caring for children it is important to recognise that the heaviest burden is likely to fall on working-class women, given that the middle and upper classes can often buy access to resources which relieve the stress of caring.

In addition to performing the bulk of informal care, research (Equal Opportunities Commission, 1980, 1982a, 1982b, 1984; Bayley, 1983) shows women are more likely than men to:

- provide the most intimate of personal care
- go on caring longer and for adults with higher levels of dependency
- give up work to look after a dependent or dying child or ill adult.

A recognition of the cycle of caring and its nature is crucial for social work assessment and planning. Stages in the cycle may overlap and women may be caring simultaneously for elderly relatives and children. The potential conflicts women face in demands for attention and around the allocation of space in houses designed for nuclear family living are familiar to most social workers both from their own personal lives and from the lives of their clients.

Caring for adults is taken to be as natural for women as caring for children. Because this view is often internalised, if the act of caring is unsuccessful, women blame themselves. The failure is personalised. In our view caring for adults, like the institution of motherhood, is socially constructed and needs analysis before it is possible for practice and services to intervene in ways supportive to women. A book appropriately called *A Labour of Love* (Finch and Groves,

1983) identifies through its various chapters the components of caring for dependent adults. They include:

1. Caring is composed of two elements: caring about a person (love and feelings for a person) and caring for them (washing, feeding, laundering, etc.). The first form of caring is concerned with emotional aspects, the second with looking after or 'tending'. As individuals we may prefer to be cared for by someone who cares about us, but in residential and day care work caring for or tending someone may precede caring about the person, or it may never happen. The same process, although we do not like to admit it, occurs in families. In certain situations such as acute sickness necessitating hospital admission, we readily accept the separation of caring about and caring for.
2. Caring for or tending is often hard and laborious.
3. Caring must go on irrespective of whether there is love in the first place or whether it continues (Graham, 1983, p. 16).
4. Caring is about keeping people alive (Graham, 1983 p. 25).
5. There are costs involved in caring for people. These can be measured in personal terms as relationships with men, children and friends are affected. Living space often becomes cramped, and social life is likely to be restricted. There are also economic costs. While employment is now the norm for women, those caring for dependent adults or handicapped children are less likely to be in work (Rimmer, 1983, p. 138). Not only does caring involve additional costs for items such as heating, laundry and food, but also the possibility of maintaining living standards through having two wages is less likely. Calculations of loss of earnings vary from £2000 to £6000 per year depending on the base used (Rimmer, 1983). The assumption behind social policy that the man is the breadwinner while the woman is available at home clearly does not now fit the facts of women's lives, but it is an assumption behind the policy of community care.

Without the sacrifices of women, community care could not possibly work.

6. There is a bias against women in the way in which community resources are allocated both to the carer and to the dependent person. Men are not expected, and do not expect, to do as much as women when caring for another or in looking after themselves. Women are expected, and expect, to do more for themselves and others than men (Ungerson, 1983, p. 47; Walker, 1987, p. 122).

7. Women predominate as informal carers. 'Correct ideas' about femininity and masculinity support sex role divisions in which caring for dependent adults is seen and experienced as a woman's duty. In spite of mass unemployment affecting the lives of many men and the fact that paid work is now a part of the majority of women's lives, women are believed to be, and often believe themselves to be, the appropriate persons to take on this unpaid labour.

Care and social policy

Even if care is given within an emotional relationship, it remains work. Social policies ignore the element of labour; for example, current social work practice is to withdraw services when an elderly person moves into the home of a relative. Social services are likely to assess the elderly person as no longer at risk. Roy Parker argues that if we are to take seriously the needs of the carer and the work of caring along with the vulnerability of the elderly person which necessitated the move, services at least should be maintained if not increased (1985).

Social policies treat the care of dependent adults, like the care of children, first and foremost as a private concern to be carried out in those places where intimate relations with women are found (Graham, 1983, p. 16). The state intervenes only in emergencies, when families or friends are no longer able to cope on their own or when there is no family. To turn to the state is to admit failure on the part of the caring woman as no collective responsibility is accepted beyond a last resort safety net. The cost is said to be too high, but no cost, personal, physical or emotional, is seen as too high for the family, in particular the women who are in the main responsible for providing care. Social work intervention is primarily aimed at supporting and monitoring women as mothers and women as carers.

The form taken by these relationships of love and work arise out of the structuring of women's relations with men.

Questions

1. Can you add to the list of qualities demanded of the 'fit mother' in this chapter?
2. Do you agree that all the qualities listed on page   are necessary or desirable to be a 'fit mother'? If you disagree or wish to qualify any of the qualities on this list, why and how?
3. Think of the children you have witnessed being taken into care. Were there economic or social factors including race and gender, as well as negative mother–child interactions in these decisions?
4. How have women in your family been affected by the cycle of care?
5. Think of your experience involving the care of dependent adults within the family. What help is given to the person who assumes primary responsibility?
6. Have you observed differential resource allocation when the carers are men rather than when women or black rather than white? If yes do you think any factors other than gender or race were involved in these decisions?
7. What qualities do you think are important for 'fit fathering'?
8. Before proceeding to the next chapter, have you any views on why women's relationships with men are so important in determining the nature of women's work?

5

Living with Men

Almost all women marry. Today approximately 93 per cent of the population marry at least once (Gittens, 1985). Almost all women have in common the experience of being a wife at some time in their lives and of being houseworkers. We share these experiences with our women clients. Living with men and caring for them is held to be the central focus of a woman's life. It is a prerequisite for caring for children as, in dominant ideology, children 'should' have fathers and preferably their biological fathers living with them. These are aims towards which many women strive; that is, to marry and have children in a nuclear family setting.

The experiences we have in caring for men, however, range from the positive through to the negative. We need, therefore, to look more closely at the expectations we have of living with men and the position of women in marriage, because social policy and social work practice are closely bound up with preserving and creating particular forms of interpersonal behaviour and relationships.

Concerns of social workers

Social workers on the Social Service Needs of Women courses said that the interpersonal problem most frequently presented by their women clients concerned their relations with men. These were primarily focused on relationships within the family, but as we shall see in Chapter 7, relationships between male and female colleagues are also problematic for women social workers.

Concern was expressed in a number of ways about the quality of the relationships women have with men in the home. Given the isolation in which many women labour in the home, the lack of a close personal relationship with the other adult living there was seen as contributing to the depression and ill health of women (Brown and Harris, 1978). When husbands are not contributing, or only doing so marginally, to the work of maintaining the home including fulfilling caring duties, the excessive workload of many women clients can have a negative impact on their physical and mental health. Violence against women was another problem identified by both probation and social service workers. A high incidence is to be expected since wife abuse is widely spread throughout all social classes (Select Committee on Violence in Marriage, 1975; Dobash and Dobash, 1980; Binney, Harkell and Nixon, 1981; Pahl, 1985; Wilson, 1983). An unknown but estimated substantial minority of men abuse both their wives and their children (Rhodes and McNeill, 1985). This, too, was raised by the women on the Social Service Needs of Women courses.

There has been a surge of interest in professional circles about the sexual abuse of young children. In the vast majority of cases the survivor is a girl and the abuser a male known to her, often in her own family (Nelson, 1987; Ward, 1984). Rape crisis and women's aid have called attention to sexual abuse as a feature in women's lives for many years (Brownmiller, 1975; The London Rape Crisis Centre, 1984). The estimate that between 1 in 5 and 1 in 10 women are sexually abused when children does not come as a surprise to these agencies. It is clear from both theory and accounts of practice that learning to survive violence and its threat is part of most women's life skills. It was high on the agenda of women social workers who were sensitive to the gender perspectives of their clients' lives and their own.

Women, too, can be violent towards others, but those who use physical violence as a means of coping in relationships are viewed as extremely deviant and, irrespective of age, are penalised accordingly. (Carlen, 1983; Carlen and Worrall, 1987). This was a small, but significant problem for probation officers in their work with women.

Although not one of the statutory responsibilities of social work, relationships with men must be a significant focus of any practice which aims to be woman-centred. But how are we to understand the lack of response by social workers to requests for help from women with problems with men? Men figure prominently in the lives of many women clients, and may even be identified as a major problem for the woman client, but social work intervention is either seen as inappropriate or as impossible. To understand why this should be so involves examining the social basis of the structuring of male–female relationships through marriage and family life (Smart, 1984; Hanmer and Maynard, 1987) and the law relating to social work.

Resources for structuring marriage relations

William Goode, an American sociologist, speaks of marriage relations as having four resources through which husbands and wives structure their relationships with each other (1971). These are: economic resources, force and its threat, status, love and friendship. In three of these men are likely to have more resources than women.

Economic resources

Domestic labour is another form of social reproduction. By cleaning, feeding, and some argue, even by intimate personal behaviour, including sexual servicing, women reproduce the labour force by enabling men to daily return to their place of work (Dalla Costa and James, 1972). In assessing household income the unwaged work of women is not counted. Christine Delphy argues that this invisible financial contribution exposes the inaccuracy of the belief that women are maintained by their husbands (1984). The so-called domestic labour debate examined how women bring the equivalent of income into the family through domestic production of goods and services (Malos, 1980). Further, when women are in paid employment their wages are almost always used on family rather than personal expenditure. When women have paid work outside the home they are providing cash for their own upkeep as well as making an invisible financial contribution through unwaged domestic work.

The wife, in caring for her husband so that he may return to the paid workforce refreshed and able to carry on another day, is contributing to the Gross National Product, although this is not counted in reckoning the amount of goods and services produced in society. This was an issue raised by many women from around the world at the United Nations Decade on Women Conference in Nairobi, Kenya, in July 1985. A resolution calling on governments to count the labour of housewives in the Gross National Product was passed by the official conference, although not supported by the British delegation.

While this development may have important psychological benefits in terms of resources between husbands and wives, domestic labour will remain unwaged. The husband will continue to be able to exercise control over his wife and her labour through the allocation of household finance (Dobash and Dobash, 1980; Pahl, 1980, 1982; Homer, Leonard and Taylor, 1984). If we look at those who are unemployed and in receipt of either unemployment insurance benefit or supplementary benefit, the man is deemed to be head of the household by the State and receives payment for himself and his wife. This also is true for those of pensionable age. In the State insurance and supplementary benefits systems women are dependent on men. Women are sometimes able to receive payments in their own right even when living with their husbands, but this is always an exception and must be applied for and agreed by the officials concerned.

Jan Pahl suggests that there are four systems for allocating money in the home: the whole wage system, the allowance system, the pooling system and the independent management system (1980, 1982). In the whole wage system the man hands over all of his wage packet, the wife manages their financial affairs which includes giving him a small amount for his personal needs. In the allowance system the husband gives his wife a housekeeping allowance which is meant for spending on specific items, such as food. It may or may not include items such as the children's clothing, gas or electricity, etc. The pooling system usually involves a joint bank account and is a 'share and share alike' method. In the independent management system husbands and wives manage their money separately and each makes payments for particular items of household expenditure.

These basic systems have been modified by the work of Majorie Homer, Anne Leonard and Pat Taylor who have examined the money allocation systems of women coming into Women's Aid in Cleveland (1984). There are two additional types of whole wage system. In one the woman receives no money whatsoever from her husband, the whole wage is his. In the other, the woman is handed the wage packet but must give back money whenever it is demanded. This was also found to be a feature of the allowance system. They report that distribution of money is more of a problem when money is short. Out of 78 families, the overwhelming majority of family incomes were controlled by men through all types of distribution patterns. In only three or four families was control by the husband not evident, as the woman had total control over her income.

There was a relationship between women's working patterns and the control of family income by men. Where men had total control over family income no women went out to work, 'a factor which apparently both aided and grew out of their husband's dominance' (Homer, Leonard and Taylor, 1984, p. 11). Alternatively, when women were in paid employment, the husbands reduced the money they gave to their wives or they expected them to take on additional financial responsibilities. Prior to coming into the refuge, 71 per cent of the women were living below supplementary benefit levels.

A few had no money whatsoever. Even their child benefit was taken by their husbands. Before coming to refuges women may turn to family for help; for example, going to their mothers for meals for themselves and their children. This solution, however, is rarely permanent and if men continue to refuse to treat their earnings or benefits as a family wage, then women can be driven into refuges. Many women in refuges express great relief and pleasure at having more money over which they genuinely have control for themselves and their children once on supplementary benefit in their own right.

Once on social security, however, women's economic problems can take another form. The threat and practice of cutting off supplementary benefit, of being monitored and questioned by social security officials, is a persistent worry for many women. Women who are thought to be cohabiting with other men will lose their incomes. The danger of this can restrict an already socially isolated woman from forming new relationships.

Force and its threat as a resource

While Goode saw the use of threat and force as a last resort resource, that is to be used only after all else failed, this is not the correct way to understand this factor. Men may use the threat of force, and force itself, independent of the acquisition of other resources and in preference to gentler methods of control. This may be linked with an understanding of masculinity, i.e. of what being a 'real' man is about, or it may be simply that as husband he can get away with the use of force provided he only attacks his wife.

Rebecca Emerson and Russell Dobash speak of wives as the appropriate victims of violence (1980). In a study of police response to violence between husbands and wives in Scotland, they found that 75 per cent of violence in the family was wife assault, while 1 per cent was husband assault; 45 per cent of all violent assault was within the family. These statistics are unlikely to accurately reflect the amount of violent assault in the family relative to violent assault in public. The police are less likely to act if assault occurs in the home between people known to each other (Stanko, 1985), and there is considerable under-reporting of these offences (Hanmer and Saunders, 1984, 1987; Radford, 1987).

While we do not know the amount of force and its threat used in marriages, our understanding of its pervasiveness has expanded greatly since the early 1970s. At one time violent assault in marriage was thought to be very unusual, although social workers were always more aware than the general public of the extent and type of violence women may experience in marriage. However, the latter half of the nineteenth century was a time of widespread knowledge about the abuse of women and girls in Britain. Campaigns and concern focused particularly on the vulnerability of women in or accused of prostitution, on domestic service as an occupation and on relations in marriage (Jeffreys, 1985). The physical and sexual abuse endured by women in all three of these situations was seen to result from their social and legal statuses and not to be a problem suffered by a few inadequate or abnormal individuals. Considerable effort went into effecting legislative changes that gave women the same rights to state protection as enjoyed by men.

It seems that the knowledge of violence to women as a social issue dwindled with every legislative victory. From 1882 onwards women gradually gained control over their own earnings and inheritances. The extensions of women's rights, although initially very limited, to separation, divorce, maintenance and the custody of children, changed many aspects of marital relations. The age of consent was raised from 12 to 16, and last of all, the law on incest was passed in 1908 (Hanmer, 1983; Coveney *et al.*, 1984).

The right to vote was the last reform to be achieved by the first wave of feminism and, in the agitation just before World War I, there was a resurgence, although smaller than in the latter half of the nineteenth century, of public consciousness about violence to women. Votes for women were seen as a way of accomplishing many aims, including the control of male violence. It was believed that a fully enfranchised female population would ensure the legislation needed to enable all women to have a decent life.

The lowest point of public consciousness about violence to women was reached in the period immediately after World

War II. When conscious knowledge was at its most restricted, the social aspect of the problem was lost, and violence was redefined as the problem of a few individual deviant people, and possibly the problem of certain social groups. As the problem became located in the personalities of women, few professional workers saw the abuse of women as requiring that they take action to protect the victim. They thought that the women should learn to stop precipitating the violence. These attitudes remain with us today.

A study of a town in the North of England shows that social workers may not think physical and sexual attacks on wives are major problems in their marriages (Maynard, 1985). While this random study of case records found that violence to wives was mentioned in one-third of those examined, other factors were seen as 'the problem'. Violence to wives was ignored as a causative factor in the problems of families and as a cause of the suffering of women concerned in almost all cases. Wives were given advice such as 'don't argue with him too much', and reminded that 'accepting the consequences' was necessary in marriage (Maynard, 1985, p. 130). In only 12 per cent of the cases was physical abuse seen as central to the problems of the woman and her family. It was only in these three families that the social worker felt obligated to visit because of the man's violence to the woman.

Status as a resource

In these responses we can see what is meant by the statement that men have a higher status in society generally, including in their own homes, simply because they are men. Their higher status is reflected publicly in their greater exercise of political, social and economic power. Public life is seen as appropriate for men; the woman in a position of power and authority in public is recognised as unusual if not seen as deviant. This social authority men bring into their marriages. As William Goode explains, in the working class men demand preferential treatment because they are men, while in the middle class men demand preferential treatment because they are professional (1963). What men do, think and feel, is more highly valued and hence must be taken into account with a seriousness that is denied to women's labours, ideas, and emotional responses.

Love and friendship as a resource

Love and friendship, the sole resource women are more likely to have more of than men, are gained by life-long devotion to men, children and kin. The subordination of women is rooted in their servicing role by living through and for others. Yet at moments of crisis, the affections of others may be there to sustain the wife's point of view. This resource, however, is double-edged. It is all a woman can hope for, yet once received and given, it confirms a woman's subordinate social position. Through love of husband, home and children, women are inducted into a relationship characterised by dependency on the male (Hanmer, 1978; Leonard, 1978, 1980). In this way love, too, becomes a mechanism of control of women by men.

Relationships of deference

All four resources are present even when styles of marriage vary. Men and women may attempt tò share all aspects of married life so that there is minimal role division between them, or role differentiation may be total, so that what a man does a woman does not do and vice versa. That these two extremes are not true opposites may not be evident until something goes wrong in a relationship when, for different reasons, and in different ways, women can find themselves at a disadvantage in relation to their husbands.

Both patterns are subject to the same status differentials between men and women although the implications of this are expressed differently. With shared roles women are more likely to carry greater responsibility for how the sharing is to be organised, for example, who is to pick up the children from school or stay at home with them if ill, while with highly differentiated roles women undertake activities defined as less prestigious because women do them. In both situations women are likely to undertake more work than the men with whom they live.

The term deferential dialetic is used to characterise relationships between husbands and wives (Bell and Newby, 1976). Status differentials underpin deferent behaviour as does the actual power to enforce it. The acceptance of the status differentials that inhere in being male and female makes the deferent behaviour of wives to husbands seem 'normal'. Both men and women may share the same values. An excellent example of how husbands who fail to live up to these standards are dealt with by other men was provided by Anne Whitehead who observed marriage relations in a community in Herefordshire (1976). 'Normal', that is, 'good' marriages involved role differentiation and restrictions on how and with whom women spent their time. The men, observed in a pub setting, used joking behaviour with each other to enforce behaviour deemed correct towards wives. The greatest offence was for a husband to not exercise sufficient authority over his wife.

The expression of deferent behaviour may vary between marriages. For example, a woman may be allowed to go out to a previously agreed place, such as to her relations, provided she, or someone else, provides or leaves her husband's tea in the oven. Women often interpret this type of response from their husbands as positive; as an indication of a 'good' husband. But the husband may not permit his wife this latitude. In this example from Coal is our Life, the husband threw away the food prepared by another woman. 'J. B. boasted afterwards that he had no complaints about the food, but he had thrown it "straight to t' back o' t' fire", and when his wife arrived she was forcibly told that he had married *her* and he was going to have his meals cooked by *her* alone – and he stood over her while she cooked a dinner, three hours later!' (Henriques, Dennis and Slaughter, 1956, p. 182).

Women who become active in community groups may have to devise various strategies to obtain time away from home. A creative example of outwitting a husband comes from *Women in Collective Action*:

> Even Sian, despite feeling a lot more confident generally, often wouldn't tell her husband that she was going off to a meeting. That was why she was always appearing everywhere in her slippers – if he saw her put her shoes on, he (Henriques) knew she was 'up to something'. Often, even now, she won't know until the last minute whether she can go to a meeting, or on an outing somewhere. She won't tell her husband what she is planning, she will just play it by ear, then tell him she's off up to her mother's and won't be long. She even chaired a public meeting in another town once in her slippers. She even went up to the House of Commons wearing her slippers! (Curno *et al.*, 1982, p. 24).

Other examples are provided by a study of women and their use of leisure in Sheffield (Green, Hebron and Woodward, 1987). This study found that the refusal by men to contribute to domestic tasks and to co-operate with child care arrangements were two of the most commonly experienced means by which men effectively restrict the access of women to time and space for leisure. By refusing to participate in this work men were able to regulate the movements of women outside the home and the ways in which time is spent inside the home.

The researchers particularly note that in the range of strategies men use to regulate the behaviour of women in the home, playing on women's guilt feelings is a particularly prevalent form of control. As one woman said 'you feel guilty sometimes, don't you, because you've actually not ironed or not cleaned up or not read to your child in order to get an hour to yourself' (p. 84). Other strategies range from petty forms of behaviour, sulking or 'having a face on' through to the explicit exercise of male authority by forbidding the woman to go out. This can be backed up by threatened or actual violence. Thus the restricted access of women to public space both enables men to control the way women use time in the home and outside it.

Even though there is some individual variation, a wife does not have the same legitimated authority to limit her husband's time away from home, whether spent with his mates after work in the pub or in other company or another place (Whitehead, 1976). Nor does a wife have the same authority to enforce how her husband uses his time when at home. Men can set limits to the freedom of women with whom they live, either overtly as 'you may not' or 'other women can, but not my wife', or more covertly so that a wife indirectly seeks permission through some form of consultative process with her husband.

Divorce: reformulating marriage

Divorce is not so much the absence of marriage as marriage by another name (Dezalay, 1976; Delphy, 1976, 1984). Divorce regulates the financial claims wives and husbands can make on each other and when there are children it regulates access, custody, care and control, and guardianship. The only right that is extinguished on divorce is that of sexual access. With separation or divorce women can remain, or can become, in great danger from ex-husbands or ex-cohabitees. It is when relationships break down completely that some women experience their greatest problems with men. It is only when there are no children and no on-going financial payments that divorce truely can be seen as legally extinguishing a relationship rather than legally constituting it in a new form (Carew-Jones and Watson, 1985; Smart, 1984; Brophy and Smart, 1985).

Black and other ethnic minority women

Relationships with men can be a problem for women from ethnic minorities as well as for women from the dominant culture. Because of racism black women may be even more reluctant than white women to report to the police or take legal action. This can be because of black women's understanding of the differential response of the criminal justice system to black men and a fear of intensifying the pain inflicted on them by white people (NiCarthy *et al.*, 1984). They themselves may be treated unsympathetically by the police (Radford, 1987). Women are fully aware of what is happening in their communities. Because of racism black women may find it easier to speak frankly in groups where both cultural differences and racism are fully appreciated. It is important that these opportunities are available since black women may only feel comfortable in certain neighbourhoods where the people of their communities congregate and where culturally relevant services are available, for example shops with particular foods or meeting places (NiCarthy *et al.*, 1987). There are black and Asian women's aid refuges in many cities in Britain to which social workers can refer black and Asian women clients. Run by black and Asian women, they accept unmarried women who wish to leave home as well as women with children.

White social workers can be made to feel that they should not help Asian women as male control of women may be said to be an integral part of their cultures. White social workers can be accused of racism because they are said to be attacking the culture when they offer assistance to Asian women. But Asian culture, like British culture, is not monolithic. Men and women can have differing views about appropriate behaviour as can people in different social classes and from different parts of a country.

Anti-semitism operates in similar ways. A Jewish woman living the traditional orthodox lifestyle may have as many restrictions placed upon her as her Muslim sister. More assimilated Jewish women face social stigma and impending poverty like other women. It is important to remember that not all Jews in Britain are white and that Jewish women face greater social pressures to conform to the ideal family type than many women in the dominant cultural group. The first Violence Help Line for Jewish Women in Britain operates from Leeds. It offers help and advice to Jewish women, victims and welfare workers (Shifra, 1986).

Interpretations of religious teaching can vary amongst Muslims and Jews as amongst Christians. Claims that male control of women is validated by religion is, like culture, contested from within. Social workers should not be put off from meeting the requests of women for help by accusations that they are attacking religious beliefs by doing so.

Sometimes Asian women prefer to come into white women's aid. Determined to leave their homes, they accept that they may be completely cut off from their social group. Asian women who do not speak any English, who have never handled the money, who have almost never been outside their homes, have been rehoused with their children by women's aid and learned to cope on their own in a culture that many deeply fear for its racism. The fear of racist attacks can keep women from seeking help as can their fear of the British State (Cohen, 1980, 1981, 1982; Cohen and Siddiqi, 1985; Women, Immigration & Nationality Group, 1985).

Problems in social work practice

We now begin to see why social workers find it difficult, if not impossible, to respond to requests for help from women with problems with men with whom they live. The control of women in the home is so normalised that what women are complaining of is the very nature of marriage itself. The conflict social workers feel between their desire to assist unhappy, depressed and even desperate women, can lead them simply not to see or not to give much importance to aspects that deeply concern their women clients. Women may be silenced knowing that no one can help or that no one wants to help, and her problem is turned back upon her. Negative stereotypes of women, the so-called manipulative behaviour of wives, may be the survival skills of the oppressed.

Mary Maynard in her study of social work responses in a Northern England town illustrates these processes (1985). If women are seen as deviant in the way they look after themselves; for example, as slovenly, or their husband complains that she witholds sex, or he describes the home as a tip, or if he does not like the way the children are cared for, then social workers feel they can understand, even if not condone, his subsequent violent actions. This understanding comes from an acceptance of the system of gender stratification. It is accepted unquestioningly that it is her obligation or duty to serve him in the manner he views as desirable or necessary.

Another example, from the Research Group of the Women's Aid Federation (England) highlights multi-professional involvement (Women's Aid Federation England, 1984). Many women first respond to repeated matrimonial abuse by going to their doctor who prescribes tranquillisers or anti-depressants. Of these women some go on to be admitted to mental hospital and a few either attempt or achieve suicide.

The social workers, psychiatrists and others who treat these women in hospital are often unaware that their patients are having difficulty with the men with whom they live. It is not uncommon for women to remain silent about the abuse that has led to these outcomes. They may have tried to tell in the past to no effect or feel it is of no interest or beyond the power of the professionals to do anything about. Women sometimes use mental hospitals as a place to take a break when unable to cope any longer in an abusive home environment. They, and the staff of the institution, have learned to rub along with each other, neither party making strenuous demands on the other.

These feelings and behaviour on the part of women are created and maintained by professional behaviour (Borkowski *et al.*, 1983) Stark, Flitcraft and Frazier have begun to study the processes by which violence against women is turned back upon the woman by the medical profession so that she becomes the problem rather than the abuse she has received (1979). Social workers in hospitals work in a secondary setting. They have a secondary role in relation to the medical professionals which increases their difficulties in recognising and responding appropriately to violence against women.

Even if social workers do not accept this way of working as correct, given the way services are structured and rationed it is not easy to think through ways which will alter the situation positively for women. Social workers can feel frustrated and defeated by problems women bring involving relationships with men. This is not just a question of ideology. Women social workers are controlled *as women* by the male members of the client's family. Men social workers, too, are met by an unspoken belief on the part of the male head of household that a 'man's home is his castle'. To challenge his 'right' to do as he pleases in his own home may invite violence.

Social work managers are beginning to focus on violence against workers with the mentally ill and those with criminal convictions being singled out as particularly dangerous. The danger of assault is beginning to be recognised in residential, day care and fieldwork settings. Approaches include special training on how to deal with violent clients and paired visits to some homes. Social workers, too, need protection from violent and potentially violent clients, many of whom are men in families. Recognising the dangers in confronting men in families is a way of beginning to rethink practice with women who are being repeatedly assaulted or abused in other ways.

The study of social work responses to violence to wives illustrates that these patterns of interpersonal behaviour are not just questions of individual personality difference, or socialisation, or the interaction between the couple, but the expression of a system of stratification in which differential status is an emergent property of the distribution of power.

Marriage relations are not just about different socialisation, or even different uses of power, but of actual power itself. This is why problems women bring to social workers that arise from fulfilling domestic and caring functions seem so intractable.

When maintaining relationships and giving care become problematic, women's identity and self-esteem are adversely affected.

Questions

1. Can you think of situations in which the power of men is used to control the activities of women in and out of the home?
   a. within your own family?

      b.   within the families of social work clients?

2.   How do the women concerned fight back?
      a.   what strategies for survival or getting their own way do the women in your family adopt?
      b.   what strategies for survival or getting their own way do the women clients you work with adopt?

3.   Think of each resource available in marriage in turn; that is, money, social status, threat and use of force, and friendship or love.
      a.   how is this managed within your own family?
      b.   how is this managed within the families of social work clients with which you work?

4.   Have you ever intervened or worked with a woman's husband or cohabitee? If yes, what were the circumstances? How could it be extended for use by your social work colleagues?

5.   If you have never intervened or worked with a woman's husband or cohabitee, have there been situations in which you wished that you could have done so? What were the circumstances? What changes in your agency would be necessary to enable work with husbands and cohabitees to be undertaken?

6.   Are there differences in the way you approach working with black and Asian women from that of helping white women? Do any agencies you know treat black women differently from white women?

7.   What do policies on non-racist practice mean in practical terms for black and other ethnic minority women?

6

Women, Personal Identity and Self-esteem

A central concern on the Social Service Needs Of Women courses was with the poor self-image many of the women clients have of themselves. Women were described as lacking in self-esteem, depressed, lacking in confidence and motivation. These are commonly cited problems in working with women (Burden and Gottlieb, 1987; Gottlieb, 1980; Hilberman, 1980; Rieker and Carmen, 1986; Walker, 1983). Surrounded by the problems of bringing up children, caring for adults in poverty within a context of under-resourced support services, women clients can translate this experience into a view of themselves as failures. Women who are too ill, or too physically or mentally handicapped to be able to work, clean and care for men and children may feel guilty, as may those separated because of imprisonment or addiction to drugs or alcohol. They may think of themselves as failures because they cannot or do not care for others. A lack of care provided by others, which may be expressed through physical and sexual abuse in childhood or when an adult can also result in damaged self-esteem and identity.

Poor self-esteem in women is not a simple response to negative social beliefs held by others, for example about a social class or an ethnic group, although it can be extremely painful and damaging to be dismissed in this way. To be treated as inferior because one is identified as belonging to a particular group of people is to deny the validity both of that group's culture and of oneself as a unique human being. However, the relationship between membership in a socially less valued group and self-esteem is ill understood, for example, Solomon explains that 'We need greater understanding of the mechanisms whereby some black people have strong, positive identification with their racial group while others perceive it as negative and having shame bearing associations' (1976). Making the history and culture of black and ethnic minority women visible in positive ways is important in relation to personal identity. This point holds for any despised or rejected social group, for example, lesbian women.

Nor is poor self-esteem in women a simple process of failure to reach standards set by others, for example, an inability to meet the media image of the body beautiful. The able-bodiedness basic to the media presentation of beautiful women does create particular stresses for physically handicapped women (Campling, 1981; Hardicker, 1986), as women, like men, do judge themselves against external standards. But even though dominant ideology may appear to have wiped out any dissenting views, women are not simply the passive recipients of culture. Further, the relationship of women to femininity is mediated through their group membership. Thus black and Jewish girls can be more achievement-oriented in school than the ideology would have us believe is appropriate for working-class girls in particular.

While recognising the above factors and the unexplained differences that exist between individual women, the participants on the Social Service Needs of Women courses led us to the conclusion that it is the interconnections between giving care, maintaining relationships and self-identity that is particularly problematic for women. In this chapter our aim is to explore the inter-relationship between the demands made on women rather than focusing on mono-casual explanations.

Women's identity and caring

Women's identity is not synonymous with the activity of caring for other people, and the neglect of themselves and other women except when very young or old. Rather, caring is an aspect of identity which is prominent in living our lives as women, and in the work we engage in with women in the community. The Social Service Needs of Women courses reinforced our conviction that the issue is important for social and community workers to understand more fully.

Caring is a central theme in social work as well as in the statutes governing its provision in Britain. In social services, caring is emphasised while the control elements of the social service department's work often are obscured. Social powers to curtail the liberty of people and to control where they reside are considerable. These powers affect children and young people, their parents, the mentally ill and handicapped, the elderly and young offenders. In contrast, the Probation Service has made care in the context of control a theme of academic debate and an overt part of its practice (Bottoms and McWilliams, 1979; Harris, 1980). Given the combination of care and control as a central component in social work practice and the lives of women generally, the conflation of woman with carer is crucial.

We have identified three main components that make women the legitimate carers of others.

- the different values placed on the social behaviour of women and men
- the correspondence between the skill and abilities of carers and feminine characteristics
- social policy reinforcement of sex stereotyping of the role of carer.

The different valuation of social roles

Being a wife, a mother, and giving care are seen as more important for a woman than being a husband, a father and a carer are for men. For men the roles of procreater, economic provider and worker are stressed. The 'oddity' of the single, childless woman is tied to her separateness from both men and children. She has no one but herself to care for. Living with other women is discounted as a legitimate way of caring, because whatever the reality in practice, women are not seen as in need of being looked after except when they are very young or very old or very ill.

Caring creates cohesion between the home life of women and employment even though 'Unlike the labour contracts negotiated through the cash nexus, caring is a work role whose form and content is shaped, and continually re-shaped, by our intimate social and sexual relationships' (Graham, 1983, p. 29). Caring as a work role 'provides the basis on which women negotiate their entrée into these intimate relationships and into the wider structures of the community, the state and the economy which surround them' (Graham, 1983, pp. 29–30). The paid work women are most likely to undertake involves elements of care and service.

Work involving care and service contains an emotional element even when the work is paid employment and part of the capitalist mode of production. Psychological distance has to be created so that the individuals for whom care and service are being provided are not seen in the same way as family, relatives, friends, neighbours. This is an important aspect of training for social work practice that students often find confusing and distasteful.

Our paid work is usually fitted around what we and others agree are our responsibilities for family (Finch, 1983). An expected emotional element is the distinctive feature of the work that women undertake within the family, with relatives, friends and neighbours. The fact that care of children and relatives may be given without love, does not alter the fact that it is expected to be there. As women, whether clients, social workers, mothers, wives, daughters, that is what we believe and hope will happen. In this situation psychological distance from those for whom care is provided is seen as problematic.

What are the abilities and skills required in caring?

Clare Ungerson provides the following list of abilities and skills needed for professional caring:

- time, with short notice availability, and in flexible amounts
- high levels of domestic skills, for example in cooking, cleaning, washing
- high levels of social skills, for example, in talking to their clients in order to assess their present and future needs
- skills in information gathering about other services, and an ability to manipulate other services on the behalf of the client
- ability to act autonomously over a wide range of tasks of widely differing skill levels
- punctuality and reliability
- ability to operate over long periods in fairly isolated circumstances and to engage in routine and often unpleasant tasks particularly in the case of the very old, the mentally handicapped and mentally ill, with very little measurable success let alone positive response from the client (1983, p. 64).

This list of skills is required of any one involved in the activity of professional caring, but as Claire Ungerson points out, these skills are also the 'socially expected attributes of women in Western European society, and most mothers attempt to fulfil them daily through the medium of housework and childcare' (1983, p. 64). These skills are tied to femininity. An inability to provide care, for example, when women are forcibly separated from their children because of criminality or illness or handicap, makes many women feel 'unsexed' (Graham, 1984).

In contrast, men are likely to be 'unmanned' if they enter too far into caring activities. Lorna McKee and Margaret O'Brien in a study of fathers caring for children on their own concluded, 'Lone fatherhood appeared to move some men away from their own sex, from what they perceived as the usual activities and concerns of "the average man in the streets" ' (1983, p. 155–6). These fathers actively promoted more contact with *other* women, particularly those with children because their detailed experiences and concerns were similar. Women are more likely to understand and to be able to act as a resource.

Masculinity, however, is not a unified concept. David Morgan argues that there are different socially-approved masculinities (1987). Factors such as social class, ethnicity and culture, educational attainment, to name a few, affect the detail of approved masculine behaviour as do the situations in which certain behaviours are called for, for example, in warfare. This point, of course, also applies to femininity.

But a loss of masculine identity is particularly felt when men cross over into intimate areas of care such as washing and caring for bodies and the cleaning of faeces and human dirt. These activities are core characteristics of caring identified as suitable for women. Claire Ungerson argues that this points to a line which, if crossed, threatens men's sense of personal order and that of the people with whom they are emotionally involved: 'The fact that women have a virtual monopoly in dealing with these aspects of tending can be most easily ascribed to a system of taboo in contemporary British society about the management of human excreta. I used the word "taboo" rather than "norm" in order to convey the idea that the transgressing of a system is polluting and dangerous' (1983, p. 73). While this is not the place to explore the impact of crossing these lines on a regular and even daily basis by male social workers in residential and day care work, more research is required in order for these men to continue with these essentially 'deviant' tasks and to look at the consequences for the clients themselves (Ungerson, 1983).

Women's employment and identity

Men in social work are crossing boundaries into areas of work socially defined as female. Women in employment who see their paid work contributing more than peripherally to their identity are entering male-defined territory. The knot is tightly tied between unpaid caring and women's identity. For many of us the knowledge of employment as contributing crucially to our identity remains covert, even if in a service occupation; sometimes a guilty secret to be shared only with other women in similar situations.

We often have to struggle to locate paid work as a central theme in our lives and identity. The struggle has both social and psychological elements. Social workers, like clients, share the same complicated psychological relationship to paid employment. Janet Finch suggests that there is a hierarchy – men's work, family, women's work (1983). This remains the pattern even in dual career families as the woman usually follows the man when his career requires geographical mobility, while the reverse occurs infrequently. If the energies and emotional demands of the woman's paid work become too demanding, it is seen as poaching on the rightful allocation of time to men, children and dependent adults.

Given this cultural background it is not surprising that until recently the employment of women was seen mainly negatively in the literature on paid work (Shimmin *et al*, 1981). Unlike male unemployment, which is examined in terms of its impact on health, sense of well-being, and psychological functioning, women's unemployment scarcely features in psychological literature (Callender, 1987a, 1987b).

In the practice of social work the employment of women continues to be seen as taking women away from the family; as a source of potential neglect. Perhaps social work, like the family itself, 'cannot make sense of women's unemployment because work for women is a way out of the family' (Coyle, 1984, p. 119). This may be true in the sense that women leave the house for a set number of hours and are not available to service family members during that time, but it is not true in terms of the family as an economic system. However, all too often the way sense is made of employment for women in social work practice is to see it as competing with caring responsibilities. Women's identity is expected to arise from, and rest upon, putting their families first.

What impact does this ordering of priorities have on women's identity? Ironically, the most revealing literature is focused on women's responses to unemployment. Women do not necessarily classify themselves as looking for a job, whereas a man is assumed to be. 'Few people thought of themselves as actively searching because, as housewives, they did not see themselves as out of work' (Chaney, 1981, p. 35). This does not mean that the experience of women's unemployment on personal identity should be seen as minimal. The relationship is complex and far-reaching, even if covert.

A loss of financial independence for some women caused a 'personal crisis commensurate with that which men experience over the loss of their breadwinner status' (Coyle, 1984, p. 107). The women in this study had to face isolation and boredom having lost their life outside the family. Claire Callender (1987b) has similar findings. With the loss of their job women lost not only a sense of financial security. Employment gave them personal confidence, a sense of independence, autonomy, and pride. Women, like men, miss the friendship of people at work. Women, like men, derive part of their identity from paid work, 'They derive a crucial sense of themselves through the social relations of work. Without work they are not only isolated, they are separated from what appears to be the mainstream of life' (Coyle, 1984, p. 118).

Obviously there are a minority of women who reject work outside the family and see their identity tied exclusively to the family, the home and neighbourhood. The validity of their decision is not in question. What must be challenged is the generalisation of their experience to all women. Paid work has a positive significance for women's identity. Women's self-identity arises out of all their experiences in life, and paid employment has been identified as an important factor in keeping working-class women out of clinically-defined depressed states (Brown and Harris, 1978). Why should this be so, particularly as work is culturally defined as antagonistic to women's caring responsibilities in the home? Viewed psychologically, paid work can offer an antidote to the negative impact of the characteristics our culture defines as feminine. This is as true for working-class as for professional women.

Feminine characteristics

The stereotypical list of 'feminine' characteristics includes
dependence, submission, self-denial, obsequiousness. Research shows women to be less confident and to exhibit less
mastery than men (Gottlieb, 1980). Claire Ungerson's list of
tasks suggests that the ability to care is rooted less in being in
control, in having power to order one's own life, than in
responsiveness, the capacity to be flexible and to either
delay meeting or to ignore one's own needs or interests.
Women talk of feeling out of control of their lives (Gottlieb,
1980); a problem for women clients recognised by the
participants on the Social Service Needs Of Women courses.

Jean Baker Miller argues that woman's capacity to care is
based in her subordinate position to men. Women 'become
highly attuned to the dominants, able to predict their
reactions of pleasure and displeasure . . . Here . . . is where the long story of "feminine intuition begins" ' (1976, p.
11). This is not to argue that women have no power in
relation to husbands and children. But power over children,
as Jean Baker Miller argues, is based in inequalities which
end when the child grows to adulthood (1976). The power of
the parent diminishes with the child's increasing capacity to
make decisions for her/himself. The House of Lords judgement in the Gillick case over the prescription of contracept-
ives to young women under 16 without their parents' consent
is an example. Power to influence husbands is of a different
order.

Women's powers over men depend on their ability to
manipulate. It is covert not overt (Gottlieb, 1980). His
position of power is permanent. He may choose to give up
some of it or all of it, but 'the equality of the "equal"
marriage depends on the man's refusal to use the power
society has given him' (New and David, 1985, p. 232). It is
equality by grace, not by right. The differential privilege of
the male in relation to the female cannot be resigned; it can
only be unused as it is legitimated by society. Equality in
relationships can be removed either temporarily when in a
bad mood or in a crisis or permanently by a man's unilateral
decision. Even if equality remains the dominant mode for

the relationship both man and woman are aware of the 'sacrifice' which he has made in terms of power lost and power gained. Both man and woman are reminded in their day-to-day actions, as well as by social acquaintances, of their personal and social deviancy.

To function effectively as carers, women must limit their horizons to the home. Women must give the home priority over all other activities, in spite of the fact that, as we have seen, women contribute earnings to the family income that help to keep a substantial number out of poverty. Naomi Gottlieb argues that a consequence of prioritising the home is that 'Many women have been socialised out of their skills and abilities', so that they will probably have difficulties in coping alone (1980, p. 18). She thinks the concept of 'learned helplessness' developed by Seligman (1975) and the negative self-evaluation this involves is crucial in understanding depression in women and, more generally, their lack of confidence and their underestimation of the value of their activities and capabilities.

Individuals can approach their own actions and life circumstances with the expectations of failure; with no hope of making any impact on changing their own life or situation. Naomi Gottlieb argues that as learned helplessness is learned we can unlearn negative responses towards and evaluations of ourselves (1980). The cost of doing so may mean losing characteristics that are based on 'giving up all sense of achievement and autonomy'; that is, characteristics believed to be feminine.

Being dependent is paradoxical for women. 'Their dependent status as housewives, mothers, dutiful daughters – is not absolute, but is conditional upon their being simultaneously depended on by others. Thus for many women, being dependent is synonymous, not with receiving care, but with giving it' (Graham, 1983, p. 24). A further irony for a mother of a handicapped child is that the dependency of children on her is supposed to end, because 'a successful mother brings up her children to do without her' (Oakley, 1974).

The problem with so much of this type of analysis is that it leaves us as women feeling foolish. We find ourselves unable to get out of or alter actual situations which are so clearly negatively defined in theory. We are rendered incompetent or become the victims of social constructs that present women as powerless and without control. A view of women as victims does not help us to move forward, to take action either on our behalf or on that of women clients. Though there are no easy solutions to the paradox of women's dependency, there are other ways of thinking which may help us both in understanding and in devising effective interventions.

Women, caring and personal identity

In *In A Different Voice*, Carol Gilligan investigates the way women define themselves and what they consider to be moral behaviour (1982). Psychology is largely written and researched from the male perspective who define women as deviant even though women are over 50 per cent of the population. Broverman *et al.* conclude that psychiatrists and clinicans see stereotypical male characteristics as mature and stereotypical female characteristics as immature (1970, 1972). Gilligan argues that we need to hear the different voice of women.

In her research men and women defined themselves differently. The women talked in terms of their relationships to and with others, 'depicting their identity *in* the connection of future mother, present wife, adopted child, or past lover' (Gilligan, 1982, p. 159). Those who achieved success in terms of academic work or employment did not see this as contributing to their identity, but rather 'as jeopardizing their own sense of themselves, and the conflict they encounter between achievement and care leaves them either divided in judgement or feeling betrayed' (1982, p. 159). Morally responsible behaviour concentrates on 'giving to', 'helping out', 'not hurting'. The standard set is the 'ethic of nurturance, responsibility, and care' (Gilligan, 1982, p. 159).

In contrast, in considering how men understand morally responsible behaviour, Gilligan writes, 'Although the world of the self that men describe at times includes "people" and "deep attachments", no particular person or relationship is mentioned, nor is the activity of relationship portrayed in the context of self description . . . the male "I" is defined in separation' (1982, pp. 160–1). One of the consequences of this is that in the USA, at least, friendships between men are a rarity.

Gilligan argues that the different perspectives of women and men mean that each is guided by different ideologies. For women, 'attachment is supported by the ethic of care', while for men 'separation is justified by an ethic of rights' (Gilligan, 1982, p. 164). She concludes that women should be working towards an understanding grounded in the knowledge that 'the absolute of care, defined initially as not hurting others, becomes complicated through a recognition of the need for personal integrity' (Gilligan, 1982, p. 166). This means that women need to claim spaces, to shift at least some responsibility for caring, but for this to happen men, too, must adopt the ethic of care.

Social policy says women must cope

Major changes cannot take place simply through the actions of individuals, including social workers. There is an assumption in social policy that women are the carers and that women must cope. 'I'll manage' is an expression which echoes throughout our childhood recollections of our mothers. The assumption is so strong that it is well nigh impossible for social workers to discuss the option of not providing care with women clients. The structure and level of services is based on an assuption that most care is provided by family and friends.

This backdrop to social policy is crucial in understanding women's experiences of being carers and social worker's problems in working with women in supportive ways. These include enabling women to decide either not to care for others or to claim more space for themselves. The Conservative Administration headed by Mrs Thatcher is not qualitatively different from previous Labour or Conservative governments in the emphasis its social policies place on the care of others expected of women. The boundaries are being more tightly drawn: 'The statutory services can only play their part successfully if we don't expect them to do for us things we could be doing for ourselves' (Thatcher, 1983, p. 215).

The 1960s is seen by the New Right of the 1980s as the period in which the advance of women's rights distorted women's relationships with men and undermined the family. Describing the 1960s Caroline New and Miriam David say that 'any commitment to equality through the welfare state was a commitment to social and economic equality between families, not within them' (1985). State commitment to sexual equality was in relation to men's and women's public lives, to their status in paid employment, and not to their relationships within the privatised family.

There are short- and long-term actions that social workers can take. Long-term solutions depend on our taking action in forums outside social work. Within social work the focus must be on 'specific practical ideas and information on ways to serve particular women – ways that can be used, right now, to solve problems, change situations and improve lives' (Gottlieb, 1980, p. xii).

Recognising women as survivors

The family is the major location of personal and social control of women. Defining women as being out of the control of their families is related to what is expected of women at different times over the lifecycle. Girls and young women are deemed out of control through a variety of behaviours that make their achievement of the role of wife and mother problematic. Being sexually active is frequently cited as a problem. Once married, women are deemed out of control through behaviours that interfere with caring for others (Hutter and Williams, 1981). This can be expressed through substance abuse, e.g. alcohol or drugs, or through criminal activities, e.g. shop lifting, or through hetero or homo sexuality, or through housekeeping and services to husbands and children, e.g. dinners not prepared or on time, house not clean enough, refusal to satisfy husband sexually, children left on their own or not given enough attention, or through deliberately harming husbands or children, e.g., in particular, child abuse. Women also are deemed out of control simply by not living with men. Being a lesbian, a mother in a one-parent family, living alone, are all ways of living that interfere with caring for men. When elderly or widowed, women are once again seen as outside the family or creating problems for the nuclear families of their children.

In terms of self-esteem and identity, however, these ways of living and relating to others can be good. Rebellion and resistence can lead to or be expressions of a stronger sense of self and self-worth. Single women, for example, have better mental health than married women (Bernard, 1972) and the demands made of women through the family can lead to breakdown and personal disintegration, as well as lowered self-esteem and an undifferentiated self (Chesler, 1972; Howell and Bayer, 1981; Penfold and Walker, 1984).

Being a woman has different meanings for women at different times in their lives. Women work on issues of identity and self-esteem throughout life. These are not developmental aspects, like learning to walk, for example, that once realised need minimal or no further effort to maintain. Not only do the specific forms taken by the expectation of others, including society as a whole, vary, but just when a woman may be feeling strong and content, life-events such as bereavement or abuse within the family can create vulnerabilities. Women negotiate their way through life. Personal integrity and identity are not static qualities. The survival behaviour of women is crucial in creating and maintaining a sense of self and self-worth that enables women to continue to meet or alter the demands made upon them (McNeill *et al.*, 1987; Women in Mind, 1986).

Survival behaviour alters over the life span because what is demanded of women varies with their age (Allat *et al.*, 1987). Survival behaviour is also affected by important differences between women, such as social class, race or specific life events, for example, the death of a child or debilitating illness early in life. Women are survivors, not merely victims upon whom the world acts. In the act of survival lies a reassessment of self-worth and a reintegration of self-identity.

Survival involves more than perserverance or living a life of quiet desperation; it means assertion, however unobtrusively this may be expressed. Survival means taking on what has to be confronted, preferably in your time, on your grounds, around your issue. Women social workers are involved in these processes as well as clients.

One way of moving forward in practice is to focus on women's identity, self-image, and self-esteem. It means tackling how women can begin to see themselves as capable of standing alone, of recognising that they have rights as well as responsibilities, and of demanding resources as well as giving service. These also are issues for women social workers who cannot do this work with clients if they do not perceive its relevance to themselves. Therefore, we next explore issues around raising consciousness of gender in the workplace. We begin by looking at the conditions of employment facing women social workers.

Questions

1. How many of the women you work with would you describe as depressed? How important do you think the following are to your women clients' personal identity? i) caring functions undertaken by them ii) living with men iii) paid employment.

2. What variations, including cultural, do you observe in the importance of caring, living with men, and paid employment to the personal identity of your women clients?

3. Do you agree that living with other women is socially discounted as a legitimate way of caring. If yes, do you think this is right?

4. How do the abilities and skills (identified on page 87) required in caring affect your women clients' lives?

5. Have you observed the 'feminine' characteristic of dependence, submission, self-denial, and obsequiousness in your women clients? Do you think these qualities and behaviours are linked to the depression and lack of self-esteem of your clients?
6. What do you think would happen if you were to work with your women clients to think through issues such as, 'Should I cope continuously?' or 'Should I be the carer?'
7. What influences prevent, and what influences promote, a positive identity for the black and ethnic minority women with whom you work?

7

Developing Strategies in the Workplace: Men, Women and Management

Team work is often seen as the means through which services to clients will be enhanced. The 'team' may refer to workers in the same office, day or residential care unit, the administrative area, or permanent or temporary groups of people from a range of professional backgrounds and training. In both interprofessional and social-worker-only teams certain differences between workers are recognised. These are located in training and priorities, in values or ideologies, and in social work methods such as the psychotherapeutic, behaviourist or other schools of family therapy. Other differences are seen as antithetical to professionalism. A professional social worker is seen as neutral and neutered, even though:

- the clientele in social services is predominantly women and in probation predominantly men
- a substantial proportion of the problems brought by women are gender-related, that is, based around mothering, caring for dependent adults, relationships with men and personal identity
- there is covertly-achieved occupational segregation at the workplace, with men grossly over-represented in management positions and with women in the lower social work grades and having lower levels of training (Central Council for Education and Training in Social Work, 1983)

- men are in gender-deviant work in direct practice, particularly in residential and day care.

Gender is rarely 'picked up' or 'tuned into' as a significant dynamic in worker–worker or in worker–client relationships. There is no academic language, no words to describe these processes. Empathy and sensitivity are personal qualities and behaviour characteristics, not the act of 'picking up' or 'tuning in' itself. The exception is in situations in which the gender of the client is likely to present a sexual threat to the worker or to other clients, but more often than not there is silence on gender in discussions about teams and how they work.

Problems identified by women social workers with male colleagues

We think that the assumption that gender is not an issue in social work is harmful to men as well as to women social workers and women clients. Participants on the Social Service Needs of Women courses said that many men relate to their women colleagues in social work, to secretaries, and domestic and administrative staff in terms of gender stereotypes. Once expressed, this concern invariably moved on to these questions:

- If our male social work colleagues make us feel undermined, incompetent, over-emotional, patronised, how do they relate to women clients?
- If this is how our male social work colleagues see us as women, how do they see their women clients?
- What messages are women clients picking up about themselves from our male social work colleagues?
- Are our male social work colleagues reinforcing learned helplessness and negative self images in women clients rather than recognising and building on strengths and sources of empowerment for women?

It is our conviction that the most likely answer to these questions is that women clients as well as women workers pick up the same messages. Both read the non-verbal cues. When the verbal and non-verbal cues contradict each other, women still hear and respond to non-verbal messages (Argyle *et al.*, 1970; Spender, 1980).

Imbalances in power make lower status people more attuned to negative non-verbal messages. Communications between social workers and clients are not between social equals. In direct practice the imbalance of power between men social workers and women clients is particularly marked. Being male, in and of itself, gives higher social status than being female. If for no other reason, this makes for the greatest imbalance of power to be between men social workers and women clients.

The power imbalance between women social workers and women clients is invariably less. Whether wanted or not, male social workers carry a socially vested authority denied women as a sex. This is not to say that women never have authority over clients, as other factors shared with their male colleagues are also important in establishing this social distance.

The position of men in the agency hierarchy and often their race and class must be added to the power inherent in being male. All these factors make it harder for women to discount a man's sexist behaviour or attitudes. Combining gender difference with race and class increases and complicates the power relationships between workers and worker and clients. In Chapter 2 we raised the complex interactions of these dimensions between workers and clients. They are no less significant in worker–worker relations.

These power imbalances may explain why social work makes scant, if any, reference to sexual harassment as an issue for women social workers. The literature on sexual harassment as a problem for working women is extensive (McKinnon, 1979; Farley, 1980; Sedley and Benn, 1982; Hadjifotiou, 1983). The TUC produces guidelines defining sexual harassment and sets out the principles upon which grievance procedures should be based. A number of unions, including those recruiting in social work, have their own policy statements on sexual harassment.

In contrast to the silence in social work books and journals, all forms of sexual harassment described in the TUC guidelines were a significant concern of the social workers on the Social Service Needs of Women courses. These findings are confirmed by those of a colleague providing assertiveness training for women in the personal social services (Sears, 1986). Sexual harassment is not confined by time or place or the position a woman occupies in the hierarchy.

Promoting men – excluding women

Working in an organisation staffed largely by women is not a disadvantage to the promotion of men. The USA National Manpower Council observed that the best way forward for a man to ensure his advancement is to prepare for a field of work in which the majority of the employees are women (Kadushin, 1976). This is because only men are taken seriously as competitors for management positions and there are relatively few of them for each to compete against.

Obviously there are women in senior positions in the personal social services, in the professional associations and in the unions, but they are the exceptions. This depressing pattern also occurs internationally today as well as in the past (Abramowitz, 1985). Apart from a temporary period following the Curtis Report in 1946, when the appointment of women as chief officers for the newly formed children's departments in local authorities was proposed and agreed, men have predominated in the management of social work. At the time the children's department was an exception within the welfare services in local government. The special position women enjoyed within children's departments was shortlived as these posts disappeared with the reorganisation prompted by the Seebohm Report (1968).

In the 1980s and for the foreseeable future, men will be managing women social workers and men will be making policies for predominantly women clients, while women will be responsible for carrying out these policies in monitoring and controlling the behaviour of women (Popplestone, 1980, 1981; Community Care Supplement, 1986). This will be so even though women in Britain as well as the United States played an important part in the development of social and community work (Walton, 1975). The past in social work is often conceived of as middle-class ladies administering to the poor, but this is a fragment of a scene in which men played a managing and dominant role. Men have always predominated in the management of organisations and in policy-making in social work. Yet women are held to be responsible for holding back the professionalisation of social work (Kadushin, 1976), and for its lack of radicalism.

The development of community work displays another pattern of the exclusion of the influence of women from social work. Women were the initiators of the new wave of community work in Britain in the 1960s, but this history is all but lost. Community work is now defined as more of a man's area of social work than a woman's world. The women pioneers are forgotten and unacknowledged (Hanmer, 1979). As with individual and family work, the participants in community work are more likely to be women than men.

The reasons women throughout the labour market are not holding management jobs in any number are complex (Walby, 1987). They include the persistence of the belief that the male should be and is the sole breadwinner in the family even though this is not true in the majority of families in Britain. In common with women generally, a number of women on the Social Service Needs of Women courses were the main wage earners because they were single women, or solely responsible for children, or the man they were living with was unemployed or on low pay. Unemployment rose steadily throughout the 5 years we ran these courses and women increasingly reported conversations with their social work colleagues in which the view was expressed that women should be the first to go if unemployment threatened.

One implication for women, irrespective of the economic, social and personal place of work in their lives, is that where jobs are thought to require both stability over a period of time and the ability to put jobs before all else, assumptions about women and their hierarchy of priorities are likely to be part of the interviewing panel's hidden agenda (Fogarty, 1971). Since management often believes commitment in both these ways is required, men are more likely to be attractive as candidates. Men are thought to be able to combine successfully both career and family. Indeed being married is an advantage to men in the search for promotion. The opposite holds for women in social work (Popplestone, 1980, 1981) and in other occupations (Hennig and Jardin, 1978).

The employer's focus on a potential conflict between child care and domestic responsibilities is illustrated by a National Union of Teachers survey in which 41 per cent of women applicants for teaching jobs were asked questions about their child care arrangements (1980). This is in spite of the fact that the Sex Discrimination Act makes this type of questioning invalid. The existence of a continuous employment record does not appear to eradicate the question of future commitment from potential employer's minds although in the intervening years the forms this take may have become more subtle. Small wonder then that the training of interviewers and selection methods are major priorities for the many local authorities with equal opportunities policies aimed at overcoming discrimination on the grounds of race or gender.

Women are more likely to find themselves in jobs where they are more easily replaced even though research on the differences between men and women workers shows the invalidity of these covert judgments:

- there is a higher turnover of both male and female employees in lower grade jobs, but in the case of clerical work, this is higher for men than for women, at least in the UK
- if grade of job and quality of the job are controlled, the differences between men and women disappear
- evidence from the UK, USA and Canada indicates that differences are disappearing between men and women in time lost from work because of illness (Holland, 1980).

Being a woman is a disqualification

Candidates will make decisions about what to reveal or emphasise on an application form or in an interview, but the choice of disclosure of gender or colour is not possible. Self revelation is inevitable, if not on the application form then immediately the candidate walks into the room. Hunt found that most of the people in her survey on management attitudes to the employment of women began with the view that apart from catering and domestic work a woman is likely to be inferior to a man in respect of the qualities considered important (1975). Even if a man and woman were considered to have equal abilities the man would be employed. Equal opportunities legislation, in particular the Sex Discrimination Act 1975, has not modified these opinions and actions in any significant way, as the proportion of women in management has not improved.

An area of debate on the courses was whether women should or should not apply for management posts and what were the consequences of doing so. The argument for applying was that if gender is an important dimension in practice, service delivery policy and management, then women should be applying. Most women on the courses had not applied. Ruth Popplestone found the same reluctance, as only 3 per cent of women in her survey had applied for promotion in the past year as compared with 14 per cent of men (1980, 1981). When she asked 55 men and 55 women respondents why they thought so few women were in management, 82 per cent said because women did not apply; 78 per cent because men are more likely to be appointed, 34 per cent because women need to be better qualified than men to be appointed. A National Association of 3 Probation Officers survey, however, (Wells, 1983) found that if women applied they stood an equal chance of being appointed, but did not examine the reasons women did not apply.

A number of women on the courses had made a conscious decision not to seek promotion. They thought that being a manager meant losing contact with direct practice, with other women, and required the development of characteristics they did not value. 'Ruthlessness', 'making decisions which ignored people's needs', 'cost cutting and rationing resources', 'getting people to do more than they thought they could cope with', were seen as negatives, but the problem of additional stress on women workers is not resolved by non-promotion.

While management styles and objectives vary, as does competence, we were told that some supervisors cut off from the pain in clients' lives. The worker, unable to share and thereby receive support from her line manager, is left on her own with the loss and grief of her clients. In our experience this unshared pain and a model of management which emphasises control, as opposed to the development of the social worker's potential, strengths and abilities in a support-ive environment, plays a major role in creating job dissatis-faction. People in high-risk emotionally-demanding work need a supportive management style. In effect we are all participating in the application of forms of management to the personal social services that are more appropriate to the industrial financial world. However, even there more pro-gressive firms are concerned about their workers, because it pays off economically.

What happens to women in management?

A common concern expressed about women managers is that they will not be accepted by those they have to supervise, but this concern is not borne out by the research (Holland, 1980) nor was it raised as an issue by practitioners on the courses, even by the few older women who had been promoted. But management, like all other aspects of social life, is not gender neutral, it is a masculine environ-ment. This is not simply a matter of male predominance, but of male culture. Ruth Popplestone found management fre-quently described as inhuman, having correct administration as its priority, emphasising the importance of procedures, bureaucratic, concerned to maintain the hierarchy, and withholding information (1981, p. 15). She contrasts male values with the female values seen to operate at the level of practice (1981, p. 12). Participants on the courses com-mented that the tiny minority of women in management had to fit in with this male ethos and way of working and some were described as 'male women'.

Women in management face a 'double jeopardy'. They are the exceptions; in jobs normally occupied by men and so in a sense they should not be there. Being a leader and showing characteristics of leadership is 'unfeminine' in sex stereotypical terms. Women who become managers have to work out their position, whereas men have no gender identity problem to solve (Reed, 1983; Community Care Supplement, 1981). In contrast, men are 'deviant' in sex stereotypical terms when fulfilling the caring nurturing role of the practitioner. For black women there is a third dimension which arises from the disadvantages and low status assigned to black people in a society where power is held by white people.

Expectations of a woman manager's level of performance are often higher than for a man in the same position. This may be the result of the 'if she got there she must be good', syndrome, or alternatively, as a lower status person, i.e. a woman, she must over-perform to justify occupying a male role. This puts additional stress on women managers.

The higher up the hierarchy the more intense the isolation women managers feel from their women colleagues. They have no gender grouping in the way male managers or women direct practitioners have. They are excluded from those pre- and post-meeting discussions in those male designated spaces of the pub and the men's lavatory. Men do not have to cope with experiences such as answering the telephone and being mistaken for their secretaries or being ignored in meetings. Men do not need to develop the necessary social skills to deal with situations of isolation and claiming the power of the position they held (Bernandez, 1983).

One way of remedying some of the problems that flow from deeply-rooted power imbalances between men and women workers in social work practice is to develop strate-gies for the work place. Antidotes are needed to feeling overwhelmed by our own analysis and being absorbed into a despondent powerlessness. Collective thinking is empowering. Sharing of experience, including survival tactics, is one way of learning faster than each of us can through our own individual experiences. Becoming more gender conscious facilitates identifying and sustaining changes in the workplace that will benefit women. These include learning to have no greater expectations for women than men managers. But ultimately one of the changes must be a reduction in the number of men in senior management and the increase in the number of women. But how is this to be achieved?

Questions

1. What are the situations, if any, that give rise to a recognition of the importance of gender on your course/ in your agency? Is the focus negative or positive?
2. Can you think of examples from your own practice or social work placements in which a denial of gender is harmful to women social workers and clients?
3. Do the men with whom you work relate to women colleagues in terms of gender stereotypes? If there are different responses from different men, what is the most positive and what is the most negative response?
4. Do you agree with us that it is both erroneous and dangerous to ignore gender as an issue in social work? If not, why not?
5. Have you observed differences in the concerns of men and women social workers? If yes, how would you define these differences?
6. Have you any experience of women managers on your course/agency? If yes, are your expectations for them different from those of men? If yes, in what ways?
7. What do you think are the major reasons there are so few women managers including black women managers in the personal social services?

8. Do you think you will apply for promotion? If no, why? If yes, how does being a woman/being black affect your thinking about your prospects?
9. Have you experienced any problems with male managers? What are/were they?

8

Developing Strategies in the Workplace: Self-awareness, Assessment and Planning

Recognition of gender differences in relationships at work is not just another example of social workers concentrating on themselves rather than their clients. While action to make social workers more gender conscious should be directed first at relationships between colleagues and line management, understanding the gender implications of work with women clients is part of this. Consistent behaviour will be facilitated by transferring learning from one group of women, i.e. colleagues, to another, the clients. While policies define what should happen, it is only colleagues who stand a realistic chance of monitoring and effectively demanding improved conduct with women clients.

As the Social Service Needs of Women courses progressed over the four-year period ten major themes emerged. Each problem is matched by strategies for coping. The list is not exhaustive, but provides a start in specifying the ways in which gender is suppressed as a legitimate concern of social work practice.

1. THEME: 'There are no spaces to talk about gender issues'. STRATEGY: Set up or join a support group.
Groups are a major way of providing support and sharing experiences. On our courses talking about shared problems was not seen as a way of 'ventilating feelings' as described by Hollis (1965) or of 'confessing' (Raymond, 1986). Rather, it is a way of identifying common experiences within and between teams, both within social work and outside it. It is

possible to analyse experiences and think through ways of responding in groups. In the women's movement this process is called consciousness raising.

Group members may try ways of coping or tackling issues with varying degrees of success. These can be 'tried on for size' by other group members. We do not all need to start afresh each time. We can learn from each other. Strategies used by others can sometimes be directly transferred to our own context, but at other times they need adaptation because strategies must fit our own personality and situation.

Clearly change is not always possible. One of the functions of a group can be to support a woman in her feeling justified in deciding to leave a particular job or to bide her time if that is not possible. Groups can encourage women members to apply for promotion by supporting their decision to do so. Groups are also places where women can bring and check out feelings which in the workplace are deemed unacceptable, or labelled as 'over-involvement', or as a failure to be in control.

Recognition of commonalities between women as workers raises the possibility of alliances. The union is an obvious grouping which crosses occupational boundaries, but the opportunity also exists within teams to make links with secretarial, administrative and domestic staff and outside the team with other professional and occupational groups that are interested in collaborating on women's issues.

Working within the union was frequently mentioned as a means of finding support by the women on the courses. We were reminded that a number of the unions are now putting women's and race issues more to the fore, but we recognise that there are still problems for a woman in taking an active part in her union. Unions continue to be mainly run by white men, even when the membership is largely women, and attending meetings in the evening can be difficult because of women's responsibilities for dependent children and adults.

Another strategy is to form alliances with women whose priorities are different from our own. As we have identified earlier, black women's issues may be different from those of white women and at times they may choose in actions and campaigns to work on priorities for black people. But alliances between black and white women in which white women support issues black women want to fight on is a crucial way of positively recognising diversities between women, and overcoming them. Support groups are one of the bases from which solidarity can be organised.

Black women and men are even less well represented in the departmental hierarchy than white women. While access to training is improving at present, black people are more likely to be in social work positions with lower status and pay: working as care assistants, social work assistants, secretaries, clerks, caterers and domestics, rather than in the ranks of qualified social workers. Making links with women staff in posts other than qualified social work is a way of establishing more links with black women.

Joint support groups outside the team may be necessary if there are no other women who believe in putting women's needs more to the fore. This lack of consciousness of women's needs may occur because women social workers, like their male colleagues, may not question relating to women clients as only wives or mothers and in stereotypical ways. On the courses there was a clear, but reluctant, recognition that women do not always support each other and of the pain this can cause other women. Sometimes women find themselves receiving more support from male colleagues than from other women team members.

Support groups are important as parts of wider networks. Conferences and workshops can be set up where practice issues and examples, teaching and learning opportunities, and research findings can be widely and easily disseminated. This not only saves us time that we as individuals would have to spend to seek out this information on our own, but it also enables us to further clarify the meaning of the material because we are interacting with others who also need to explore the same areas. Networks enable us to make relevant contacts with women and men outside our immediate area thus opening up possibilities undreamt of by the isolated individual.

Social workers needs to be aware of their own views in order to distinguish between work that is legitimate with women clients because they are both whole persons and adults, not simply occupants of social roles, and that which is beyond the boundaries of the social worker–client relationship because each holds different ideological positions about women's place in society. Without thinking through one's own views there can be a confusion between exploring with women the range of options open to them, however limited these may be, and imposing our own views on clients. We cannot assume that we know what is right for women and how they must lead their lives. This is basic to professional social work in other situations and with other client groups and needs to be extended to women.

Support groups need to face the questions, 'What is feminism?' 'Am I a feminist?' 'What does it mean to me/us?' There is a danger that we may tie ourselves up with definitions that are exclusive rather than inclusive. We may feel that we must conform to some idealistic view of 'being a right-on feminist'. Though our stereotypes may be different from those of the media, these assumptions can be equally oppressive. When this happens no one is quite sure what criteria other women are using. The only certainty is that as individuals we are likely to, indeed almost inevitably will, fail to conform. We fear that we will not meet the standards. The ideal can be oppressive to women in groups, resulting in a fear that we shall be excluded or looked down upon for some compromise or error we are making in our lives.

It is important to 'unpack' what feminism means to us as women. Anne Oakley's analysis of the range of political positions of women in the women's movement in *Subject Women* is useful, but we each need to become clearer about what feminism means at a more personal level (1981). Otherwise women in groups can feel the need to stick to a 'party line' and be reluctant to disagree with other women even when they think it is necessary. Differences and diversities can become buried and the group then ceases to function well for at least some of the women in it.

2.   THEME: 'We cannot get a word in edgeways'. STRATEGY: Learn skills for positive interventions in meetings.
The disadvantages encountered by many women social

workers in meetings are not personal failures. Research into gendered communications shows that men interrupt women in conversations more than women interrupt men. Men are more likely than women to regard interruptions of their conversations as rude (Argyle *et al.*, 1970). Women tend to speak less often in presence of men than in all women groups (Garvin and Reed, 1983) and undertake a facilitating role in conversation. In summarising Pamela Fishman's work, Dale Spender writes, 'women are obliged to be the audience, the good listener, and to keep the conversation flowing' (1980, p. 49). Women are not expected to either control the topic of conversation or to change it. People make judgements about how much women talk by comparing women who do with the silent women in the group, not with the men and the amount of time they spend speaking.

The social power men have over women speaking means that those who break rules have to face penalties for doing so (Spender, 1980, p. 46) just as they do in other areas of social life (Garvin and Reed, 1983). Control over conversation is a use of power in social work, as elsewhere, whether consciously exercised or not. The power men have to control conversations is added to when men in the room hold the most senior status, in hierarchical terms. Further, their managerial status is anticipated as everyone knows that given the weighting in favour of male promotion, the men present in the group are more likely to become managers than the women. This anticipated status is reflected in casual, as well as formal, conversations at work. Our experience is that men talk of managerial matters anticipating their promotions long before this becomes a reality. These are reasons why simply increasing the number of women in the group as a way of altering the power balance does not always work.

Strategies for coping with these problems must include improving our confidence by developing skills which enable us to put across our points more effectively without getting angry or upset. Assertiveness training was frequently mentioned and courses are now being offered by the National Association of Local Government Officers (NALGO) and some social work departments. Learning to use emotions effectively was another tactic suggested, including redirecting feelings where they belong when these get displaced onto women. Offering to chair meetings, proposing a rotating chair, supporting other women when they try to be heard or make a point were also suggested.

Making mistakes when intervening in meetings is not a disaster. Men make them and we, like them, can recover from errors. Clearly men have a responsibility to share conversation and power more equally and to be more self-aware in their behaviour towards women colleagues in the conduct of meetings. Applying knowledge of group processes and sharing power, the stock-in-trade of group workers, would meet the issues raised by many of the participants on our courses. Unfortunately what we as social workers know about communication and group work often is not extended to our work with colleagues (Parsloe and Stevenson, 1978).

3. THEME: 'Emotion is unprofessional'. STRATEGY: Find ways of legitimating emotion for both men and women.
A very common complaint was that male colleagues were unable to show or own up to emotions. In contrast women said they were often told they were too emotional, too involved, too identified with their clients. Direct practice inevitably brings social workers into contact with the emotions of others, whether these arise as a consequence of a lack of control over the material and social aspects of a person's life, or from relationship or personal difficulties.

The way men tend to handle emotions is significant for retaining control, not only over oneself, but over others. Control over emotions is often attributed to social conditions, but 'Men who may wish to stay in control of conversations may quite accurately perceive that the disclosure of emotions lead to a reduction in control . . . Power can be retained by not disclosing while someone else does' (Spender, 1980, p. 47). Dale Spender points out that this behaviour is not the same as socialised behaviour in which men never express emotion. Their pain and feelings can be privately expressed, often to another woman who holds the secret for them so that it is not seen as 'weakness' in the workplace.

Rationality places an order, an interpretation, on life events that keeps emotions at a distance. Emotions are not logical, sequential; they are messy and patchy. Joy, sorrow, grief, love and hate are the raw material of direct practice in group care and field work. Moving into management is a way for men to resolve the incongruity between the gender expectations for masculinity and the nature of direct practice. Engaging in emotions creates a fear of losing control in men. In management the task is planning and utilising human and material resources (Popplestone, 1982, p. 14). The move into management does not create a dilemma for many men in the way it does for women who often do not want to lose contact with clients. For men losing direct contact with clients can resolve a gendered dilemma.

Many of the practitioners on the courses placed considerable importance on supervision. In common with the Social Service Inspectorate we found examples of good supervision, but common complaints were that time is often short, or interrupted, and that the focus is on crises and not on the emotional impact created on the worker through helping clients whose lives are very stressful or who are at high risk (1986). Research into work with children in care and their families concludes that painful events in the lives of clients are not being addressed by practitioners (DHSS, 1986). The researchers speculate that this may not be picked up in supervision because managers tend to move from one thing to the next and workers are left coping with the pain of the client's life alone. Without support, in the end, the worker will not be able to face the pain of clients' lives either, and the client will be left without help.

In our view the gender aspects of this issue have not been explored sufficiently, although it is at least being documented. The Social Service Inspectorate report on children at risk who are being supervised at home notes that between 54 per cent and 85 per cent of the social workers involved with these clients were women and 39 per cent to 59 per cent of the supervisors were men (DHSS, 1986). It is insufficient simply to note that women in direct practice fail to pick up clues about the emotional well-being of clients. The issue is about the pervading expectations and ethos around supervision and the nature of social work itself. With the increasing emphasis on tasks and outcome – however important these may be – there is a danger that the focus of supervision leaves out the process that clients have to go through in order to overcome self-defeating and destructive patterns.

The handling of emotions and pain was a key theme on all the Social Service Needs of Women courses. Some social workers decided to ask to change supervisor if s/he was unable to provide the support and learning needed. If this was impossible because of the way the request would be interpreted or because of the availability of supervisors, finding an alternative support system was proposed. Even if alternative support systems are covert, skills and experiences are being developed. Finding ways of legitimating emotion for both women and men are important.

4.   THEME: 'What issues shall we take up and when? STRATEGY: 'We do not have to be superwomen'.
There is danger that because of our own individual or group impatience for change we forget the struggle is a collective and long-term one. Women on the courses always reminded themselves that although they often felt isolated they were not alone. Equally critical was only taking on what we can cope with, choosing our own issue to fight on, on our own ground and when we are ready. As the courses progressed spaces in which to 'fall apart safely', that is to experience emotions, to fail to cope and to become dependent, were also seen as important. We do not have to be superwomen. As women we felt we had to resist the expectation of managers to always be able to cope. But the effects not coping had on relationships with other women who may feel let down when a woman colleague becomes ill, moves job, or leaves social work can be worrying. Yet dropping out of the struggle for a time can be an important survival technique (Alinsky, 1972). We need to be kinder to ourselves and other women.

5.   THEME: 'There is no support for women workers who are carers'. STRATEGY: Support carers.
Normal working hours do not recognise the responsibilities many women have in caring for children and dependent adults. Formal provision of care leave is rare and informal support is often the only realistic alternative. Furthermore, it is much easier to take time off or to leave early to look after a sick husband, cohabitee or child, than another woman. The responsibilities women have for women friends and the commitments of single women should not be forgotten in the concentration on families and heterosexuality.

Working with organisations that recognise caring responsibilities as legitimate demands on people's time, such as the unions or local authority equal opportunity units, is one strategy. Equal opportunity units are trying to establish leave rights for caring for sick children, more flexible working hours, job sharing, and conditions for part-time work for women with dependents that do not involve a loss of status or a decline in conditions of employment or of pay. Supporting these efforts and disseminating information about both formal and informal methods of recognising the caring responsibilities of workers is a means of trying to create and generalise local gains.

6.   THEME: 'Gender is not an issue'. STRATEGY: Put gender on the agenda.
Gender issues are rarely raised on team meeting agendas. Decisions about priorities need to be made by both team leaders and members. It is difficult to get gender considered when it is so rarely seen as a focus for social work practice or policy. If gender were seen as relevant then the identification of women workers with women clients would be valued and not seen as a failure to maintain a professional distance from the client. The same would apply to male social workers in their relationships with men clients. These identifications exist and are accepted for children and young people, but tend to become lost in work with adults.

Men who work with women clients must own the negative aspects of their own power. Most, if not all men, have had thoughts and feelings of violence towards women as well as sexual thoughts and feelings. Some will have acted upon them. As we have seen the danger of violence comes not so much from the unknown stranger outside the home as from the men within it to whom women are expected to turn for protection. The protector turned violator is the theme of sexual abuse against girls and young women. Men, not just women, have to own up to their own feelings, thoughts and actions if there is to be gender sensitive practice and policy.

The issue is not to put gender on the agenda just occasionally, but to keep it there as an integral part of decision-making in social work practice. Some women workers are already doing gender-conscious work with clients. But the tendency is to not discuss this type of practice. In some agencies the social work environment may be too hostile for openness. Elsewhere it may be possible to talk about and share examples of good gender-conscious practice by members of the team or within the department or elsewhere. Keeping up to date on research is another way of giving validity to work which puts women and their needs to the fore.

7. THEME: 'Gender-conscious practice is not validated'. STRATEGY: Provide evidence.
Workers who attempt to innovate or deviate from 'the way it is done here' often face a penalty. They have continually to demonstrate greater competence in their practice. Higher standards are often set for them than for those who offer no challenge to existing practices. That this is unfair does not alter the fact that the demand for greater competence is one of the penalties for deviance earned by those who promote change. This should not be seen as a personal problem of the individual workers but as a reaction to change.

In spite of the penalties, social workers on our courses pressed on because of the positive work that could be done with clients through gender-conscious practice. They found the following ways of making gendered practice visible:

• identifying the gender composition of client groups and studying the implications this has for practice and service delivery

- using gender-specific information to name and commu-
  nicate more effectively the impact of cuts on specific
  services
- discussing examples of good gendered practice
- raising the question of giving clients the option of
  whether they have a male or a female social worker
- putting issues that affect women on the agendas of team
  and other social work meetings; this is particularly
  important for single and older women whose needs tend
  to be neglected because of the emphasis on family and
  women with children. Our blinkered thinking can mean
  that women who have spent their lives caring for others
  may end up not being cared for themselves
- getting the specific needs of all women workers in the
  agency on the agenda, not simply the 'professionals'
- getting policies about sexual harassment accepted in the
  agency and the union; ensuring that there are adequate
  procedures for making and dealing with complaints. For
  example, does the woman have the option to turn to a
  woman rather than a man? A man may have loyalties to
  the offender or may respond ambivalently seeing his
  own past, present, or future condemned
- proposing courses on work with women clients and
  supporting colleagues who go on them
- recognising ourselves as valuable resources and finding
  ways of conveying that to management.

8. THEME: 'Women workers and clients are stereotyped'.
STRATEGY: Resist labelling.
The behaviour of women workers and clients can be interpreted in stereotyped ways. 'Over-emotional', 'unfeminine', 'all she wants/needs is a good man', 'hysterical', 'stri-
dent', 'typical woman', are some of the labels that need to be
questioned. Ways of doing this varied depending on circumstances and the person. Some women asked for evidence, some for examples, while others reframed the information so that different assessments had to be made or an
alternative considered more carefully. Some women used
the family therapy technique of mirroring the despised
behaviour. Black women are particularly vulnerable to

stereotyping. Culturally accepted expressions of anger or customary communications between older and younger members of the black community could be labelled by white workers as over-excited, or extremely subservient, or passive.

We are often less effective in countering criticisms against ourselves than our clients, so support and forward planning helps. As discrediting through labelling is a repetitive pattern, rehearsing responses helps. Redefining behaviour as bullying or pressuring is one strategy, for example when charges of 'personal inadequacies' or 'lack of commitment to the job' leads to refusals to take on additional work if a woman colleague is already under pressure.

The support of other women and alliances with men are important to make changes and to make them stick.

9. THEME: 'There are so few women managers'. STRATEGY: Apply for promotion; support other women who apply; support women managers, and do not expect them to be superwomen.
A number of women on the Social Service Needs of Women courses had decided not to move away from direct practice. There were two main reasons for this decision. Some did not think the senior social workers received adequate compensation for the amount of responsibility they carried. They could see the lack of support managers experience. It is as if women see the move up the hierarchy in single and distinct steps rather than, a progression in which problems of giving and receiving support, encouragement and training are always present.

The second reason for the decision not to seek promotion is that women could see no opportunities in management positions to support the development of skills and abilities in staff. They saw management to be more about putting pressure on staff than giving support. Staff development did not seem to be integral to social work. The Social Service Inspectorate in their report on the supervision of children at home on supervision made similar findings (1986). Staff development was interpreted as a course-based activity and not carried out through supervision on the job. The few women managers on the Social Service Needs of Women courses spoke of pressures, a lack of time, and an ethos which mitigated against the development of a climate and practice in which the emphasis was on the development of the skills and abilities of staff.

Managers rarely discussed promotion prospects with the women workers on the courses. Career counselling was noted by its absence. We were surprised that very experienced women had never had any discussions about their career development with any of their managers. In contrast, women said they could identify men in their teams and departments likely to be promoted, either because they were 'grooming' themselves or because they were being groomed through exposure to situations in which their potential for management and leadership was being tested.

Some women decided to apply for promotion while on the courses and some to support other women who did so. All were aware that promotion means greater isolation from other women, but none could see how to alter the balance of power in the hierarchy until more women become convinced that they have the ability and confidence to move into management.

Gender-conscious women do not necessarily overcome all their sexism. This became an issue for discussion when talking about women managers. Not expecting much more of women than we do of men in similar positions is an important way of not putting additional pressures on already isolated women.

10.   THEME: 'Women are perceived as less employable and less promotable than men'. STRATEGY: Build up a code of non-sexist woman-centred practice.
Codes are not rules. They are ways of setting out principles, or flagging objectives so that they can be checked and reassessed from time to time. We began to build up a code of non-sexist woman-centred practice on the courses. This is the subject of our conclusion (pp. 139–43).

Questions

1. Do you belong to a women's support group or network? If not, how would you go about setting up or joining an existing group?
2. Have you ever volunteered to chair a meeting? If not, can you imagine yourself in this role?
3. Are you experiencing supervision/tutorials in which there is space to explore the emotions generated in you by the nature of the work you are doing? If not, have you thought of turning to your women colleagues for support?
4. What issue(s) would you like to take up with colleagues, tutors/practice teachers, social work managers?
5. Do the women with caring responsibilities in your office/on your course receive any support from colleagues? If not, can you think of ways in which this might be provided?
6. Is gender-conscious work discussed in your office/on your course. If not, can you think of ways it can be put on the agenda and kept there?
7. Have you found ways of making gendered practice visible in your agency/on your course? If not, could you introduce any of the suggestions on pp. 119–20?
8. Have you found ways to resist labelling and stereotyping of women clients and social workers? If not, have you thought of joining forces with others workers in your office/on your course who may wish to do this too?
9. Do you agree that problems of giving and receiving support, encouragement and training are with you as a social worker wherever you are located within the agency hierarchy? How can you offer support to women managers/teaching staff/practice teachers?

9

Developing Woman-centred Practice: Building Confidence and Overcoming Isolation

The full measure of the problems facing women is that the ordinary events in our lives are stressful (Gottlieb, 1980). As well as having a personal component, the problems of women clients are also political, social and economic. As social workers we need to find ways of working with women which address the issues of women's unequal power, status, privilege and options. We have to find ways of working with women clients that recognise the multi-dimensional sources of their problems. To do this our approach must be multi-method (Turner, 1986). Our intervention, however, is not unproblematic. We have to recognise that the involvement of our agencies, if not ourselves, may well escalate rather than diminish or resolve problems for women.

All too often women's problems, because of their inevitability, seem not just insurmountable, but immoveable in any meaningful way. For example, as one course participant wrote:

How can the angry feelings and ambivalences regarding a mother's role that is expressed by many of the mothers I work with be contained? Women feel it is their natural role to be almost totally responsible for their handicapped children, and yet they are often debilitated by the sheer burden of this work. They would like more participation by their husbands. As the social worker I often struggle with my own views and feelings. I am aware that I may be pushing against the expectations of women, for I believe raising children should be a shared job. These situations are complicated by the strong emotions which arise if a woman wants to leave her partner, but feels frightened at the prospect of bringing up a handicapped child on her own.

The range of problems contained in this example include the nature of personal relationships as well as social expectations, economic and political issues.

We suggest that there are stages or components in moving from what seems to be a daunting, overwhelming task to more manageable ways of working; ways that enable us to begin to untangle and address the complexity of the issues facing women clients and social workers. These include:

1. preparing ourselves
2. devising principles underpinning woman-centred practice
3. making our method more gender-relevant
4. linking women clients with agencies focusing on women and their needs
5. increasing resources for women
6. ensuring that women are involved in the decision-making and policy-making processes of the agency
7. drawing up a code for non-sexist women-centred practice.

1. Preparing ourselves

How can we prepare ourselves to accept the client? One major way is to challenge our own vulnerabilities away from our clients, so that we can use these with them. A major vulnerability that we need to challenge is a sense of guilt which we may have because we see ourselves as privileged in some way. This can be an illusion thrown up to protect ourselves from knowledge of our own vulnerabilities arising out of being women in this society. Guilt can be a defence against our own sense of loss and powerlessness. Guilt can block an acknowledgement that we, too, are vulnerable in ways very similar to our clients. For instance, our vulnerabilities may arise through an acceptance of male violence or male bullying or through a fear of men. We may accept sexual harassment at work and at home as do our clients.

Course participants suggested the following ways of preparing ourselves:

- by feeling clearer about what we are doing at work
- by resolving our feelings about recording and experiencing writing as positive
- by being sure of our facts and research findings
- by developing our professional skills; if we want to challenge sexist practices in our agencies and in the courts, we have to be better not the same as other practitioners
- by taking risks in asking for space, help and support; good supervision and training are necessary
- by defining where services and policies are unhelpful to or exclude women
- by keeping up to date records within the agency of resources in the area for women.

Preparing ourselves means accepting women clients as *women*, not as occupants of the social roles of wife, mother, carer, or adolescent young woman. Our practice flows from the acceptance of the total person. Before we are able to work with women clients in this way, however, we must accept ourselves as total people. Because woman-centred practice is intimately bound up with accepting women in a male-preferring society, it assumes social workers can move beyond seeing women as Adam's rib – a secondary character – to perceiving the woman client as important in and for herself.

2. Devising principles underpinning woman-centred practice

Feminist practice is described as a perspective and not a technique (Penfold and Walker, 1984). First and foremost it means liking and valuing women, including ourselves. We can then acknowledge and use our own personal experience and that of other women as a resource. We can reaffirm what women know and can do. The most fundamental precept is *to believe the woman; to accept her and the problem she brings.* While this may sound like common sense, it is not inevitable or even usual, given that women clients often are not seen as whole persons, but as the embodiment of social roles, the fulfillers of duties to others, if seen as the client at all.

To value women, to utilise their strengths and abilities as a resource, means trying to work in non-hierarchical ways. We need to create situations, however limited, in which social workers and clients can share and learn from each other. This means recognising commonalities and differences and accepting that it is the women clients themselves who have to find ways through to viable solutions. Often the most useful supports to women clients are not ourselves, though we may create and hold open the space and provide information, but other women whose circumstances have been or are similar.

Seeing women as a resource for each other and working in non-hierarchical ways means seeing the creation of all-women groups as a legitimate and valuable means of practice. The gender of the worker and the ethnic origin or race of the worker is a significant factor in practice because racism and sexism arise out of inequalities in power and social valuations. Women social workers need to spend time with women talking about issues and experiences that are important to women. This can be an enjoyable time from which social workers as well as clients can gain a feeling of exhilaration. It can be a time in which information is exchanged about ways social workers work, about support systems, about ways of dealing with men. Clients can be accepted as competent, as having strengths and rights.

If this perspective is adopted, it becomes possible to encourage women to shed the all-pervasive guilt that burdens so many and to recognise the limits of their responsibilities. Equally we can encourage women to expect and even demand time for themselves, to have fun and to see 'treats' as a right. Too often 'treats' are not considered at all appropriate for adult women and as less appropriate for young women than young men. Like gold stars and 'A' grades, they are rarely given to women. But having space, for example, from children or dependent adults, or for young women to have fun, is not a 'treat', it is a human requirement. In part, woman-centred practice means emphasising equal sharing of resources, power and responsibility, while recognising that in our society women are socially, and often in personal relationships, subordinate so that power, responsibility and resources are shared unequally.

A theme running through the Social Service Needs of Women courses was the importance of validating feelings and emotions as legitimate means of expression and communication with others. Expressing our joys, our sorrows, our frustrations, being emotional, expressing feelings, too often leads to a negative social work assessment. The woman client who does so is seen as having a 'deficit personality' rather than as interpreting her emotional response as a positive resource (Hudson, 1986).

Feminist practice also resists pathologising women's behaviour and their sexuality. It recognises that women's problems may be caused by social definitions of, for instance, appropriate sexual behaviour for young women, rather than her personality or behaviour (Penfold and Walker, 1984). Similarly, women's strategies for coping have to be seen not as requiring treatment, but rather as 'forms of resistance and struggle' which are 'functional and positive means of coping with social injustices' (Hudson, 1986). This was written about adolescent girls, but we think it applies equally to older women. Too often, social work assessment and practice is founded on the view that women are out of control of their lives and in need of treatment. Woman-centred practice focuses on enhancing women's sense of control and of coping. At the same time it involves examining self-defeating patterns of behaviour, including how external conditions can lead some women to become self-hating, and seeks to find less damaging strategies.

3. Making our methods more gender-relevant

Since women-centred practice is a perspective and not a technique or a single method, the full range of social work approaches are available to workers. We need to retain the opportunities for women to have individual therapy, counselling, or casework because these can be a necessary first step. These techniques provide an opportunity to focus on the woman entirely; it gives her time and space for herself, perhaps for the first time for many years. She can be treated as an adult, a total person and helped to clarify her situation, her view of herself, what has happened to her, her feelings and the options open to her. While some psychoanalytic practice is profoundly damaging to women, women therapists are finding means of adapting therapy so that it is woman-affirming. this is also true for family therapy (Goldner, 1985; Osborne, 1983; Hare-Mustin, 1978; Marchant and Wearing, 1986). Many cities in Britain have a Women's Therapy Centre through which women may obtain positive help (Eichenbaum and Orbach, 1982, 1983, 1985).

Because of the tendency to stereotype women and to sexualise the behaviour and problems of young women, it is important that we check out other people's definitions of women's behaviour. Annie Hudson suggests that the fears and anxieties of many social workers about adolescent girls, for example that they are uncontrollable and manipulative, also act to constrain attempts to develop different forms of practice (1986). These fears are shared by other professionals in women's lives and are a powerful influence on the way behaviour is described and assessed. An assessment of running away from home or taking overdoses may focus solely on the behaviour of the young woman. She may be deemed uncontrollable rather than exploring the possibility that her behaviour is a response to unacceptable treatment; for example, sexual abuse. Similarly Annie Hudson suggests that the category of 'slag' is easily come by, hard to shed, and is often a determining factor in shaping a young woman's career through the personal social services (1986;

McRobbie and McCabe, 1981). Checking out information and challenging definitions becomes important.

Ways of working with women should validate women's strengths. They should reinforce how women have dealt with their situations up to now and seek to build on women's coping skills. Social workers need to form relationships that enable both the client and the worker to look at how successful the client is in problem-solving. Ways of working with women include:

- relating to the client as a woman
- assuming client oppression and lack of choices
- exploring choices and challenging where there appear to be none
- validating the presence of unhappiness in many women's lives
- recognising that some women disagree with feminist views
- finding language to describe and talk about women and their oppression which is understandable and addresses their circumstances
- concentrating on limited tasks, achievable goals, no matter how small they are.

Working with women can be difficult as well as rewarding. For instance, working with a mother whose children are in care means really trusting the mother rather than pretending to do so. If you cannot trust her, it means being open with her and recognising that the work you will be doing is that of monitoring and surveillance rather than counselling or case-work.

Groups

A primary method of overcoming the disparity in power between women clients and women social workers lies in working with women in groups. Power can be increased and shared through group participation:

– through a stress on commonalities	– power differences are muted
– by having more than one social worker	– power is diffused
– by having more than one client	– power is moved from workers to clients

Groups composed solely of women, separatist groups, have to be argued for, as co-workers and management may not understand their significance for social work practice. The primary reason all-women groups are necessary is because women have different needs and problems, and the disabilities they bring are likely to be gender-related. Also the quality of group processes is likely to be improved. In all-women groups the participants work more quickly on intimate interpersonal problems and the expression of conflict is likely to be delayed until the women have begun to trust and feel safe with each other (Hagen and Hartung, 1983).

All that research has shown about the conduct of men in mixed groups is applicable to mixed groups of clients; that is, that men control the introduction and pursuit of topics, the use of the available time, the lack of emotional content in conversations (Garvin and Reed, 1983; Spender, 1980). Women are likely to defer to men in mixed settings, concentrating on the problems men bring and responding to male perceptions of how things ought to be rather than concentrating on their own issues. Women may be totally silenced in mixed groups so that common issues in women's lives, such as sexual abuse and male violence, are unlikely to be raised or, if they are, the discussion is unlikely to be from the woman's perspective. The deference women show men in mixed groups can be overcome through the all-women's group.

Only by seeing that the abusing man is not unique in his treatment of her, that the frustrations and depression she experiences with child rearing and caring for dependent adults are shared by other women, and that accepting women as sexual beings is both frightening and a problem for men, it is possible to separate her individual responsibility from the political context in which she lives. In this way the basic principle of the Women's Movement, that the personal is political, takes on meaning, transforming consciousness and releasing the energy needed to confront problems. The absence of men should be argued for as constructive to the group process because women need the opportunities to create different and less stereotyped roles for themselves *vis-à-vis* both women and men.

In summary, separatist groups for women are positive because women can identify commonalities as well as differences in their experiences and life situations. They can share strategies and learn new ones from other women. They can confront and validate their right to feel as they do. They can learn of their right for space, to talk, to put across their point of view. They can formulate the kinds of services and support they need. They can see women as a support network and as a source of fun and companionship. They can overcome social isolation. They can experience autonomy and take the initiative.

Group processes can operate in negative ways. They can stress differences between members thereby highlighting power imbalances. More than one social worker can simply increase the power of the professionals at the expense of the group members. Groups can have excluded or passive, barely participating members. Too much stress on commonalities can be oppressive by making women fearful of revealing differences, uncertainties, and the compromises each has had to make in her life.

Yet groups can be an empowering experience for clients and social workers alike. On the courses women often began from a position of despair, of feeling powerless. Often this psychic exhaustion was paralleled by physical exhaustion. Women felt unable to effect any change, but after sharing their despair, they began to share strategies, ideas and current practice which energised everyone. Caring and supportive feelings were generated through an emphasis on commonalities followed by the recognition of diversities.

Mobilising group resources and enabling the group to recognise what they have already achieved requires a style of leadership which is non-hierarchical and which sees the leader's role as enabling and not as expert. Problems and solutions have to be put back into the group because the problems and issues causing despair come from our own lives; from the context of our own practice. This process can produce anger, because the leader is not behaving as the expert, the superwoman who has all the answers. If leaders attempt this, however, even more anger is invoked because of the inevitable unrealistic nature of any so-called solutions that are offered. This anger can be directly or indirectly expressed through sullen or passive withdrawal, or by removing oneself physically as well as mentally and emotionally from the group. The psychological effect of powerful experts is to cast group members into powerless incompetent workers/clients. A non-hierarchical mode of teaching and learning with leaders acting as enablers is basic to adult education. It is a strategy that empowers clients as well as social workers and students.

Relations in groups involve the same emotional give-and-take as in one-to-one field work practice. Negative emotions are never eliminated through repression. Repression can never be a goal of practice. The recognition of negative emotions – their acceptance – the turning around of grief, loss, anger, hatred, into a determination to rethink, replan, to change, are as much the content of group work as individual work. Achieving this form of practice begins with acceptance of the client which can emanate from the recognition of commonalities.

4. Linking women clients with agencies focusing on women and their needs

Given the structure and responsibilities of statutory agencies, one of the major sources of empowerment for women clients is to link them with agencies such as women's aid, rape crisis, incest survivors' groups and groups specifically for young women (Girls In Trouble Pack, 1986). Continued involvement may be a statutory requirement or part of an agreed work plan, but we should see our input as a contribution to, not as controlling the resources for help available to women clients. Many workers in the statutory sector find it difficult to accept this view of their involvement.

A recognition that the context in which we work has an impact on and places limitations on the way we can work and on what we have to offer can be threatening and experienced as a loss of personal power. To understand the organisational limitations of our agencies is to accept that social work is not an unambiguous helper. Our intervention can have detrimental consequences for our clients.

The potentially detrimental impact of our work is recognised in some situations; for example, recommendations for probation (or supervision) orders can rapidly push people up the tariff system. There is no good reason for us not to be aware of other ways and situations in which our intervention can be unhelpful or of limited help to women. Uncomfortable as the realisation may be, it is an important step to take in order to develop a woman centred practice. By clearly focusing on the woman's well-being, it becomes possible to involve agencies that are able to offer empowering experiences, thereby supplementing statutory involvement.

Social workers do refer clients to agencies that are seen to offer a different service, such as the health service and even welfare rights organisations. Referring women to agencies such as women's aid, rape crisis or incest survivor groups, however, means viewing the client in a different way. Her well-being becomes paramount and therefore empowering experiences become an important focus for practice. Other agencies can supplement our own work by offering a form of help unavailable in our agenices.

5. Increasing resources for women

Resources for women of all ages are limited. Because their needs are marginalised so, too, are the services provided. For example, Annie Hudson argues that while there is a public and political concern with the delinquency of young males, and a whole range of resources to cope with this, it is generally assumed that girls' deviant behaviour will be coped with within the boundaries of the nuclear family where 'good parents' will be able to ensure that their daughters meet normative expectations of adolescent femininity (1986, p. 2).

Similar statements can be made about women and their needs in all the areas meriting social work concern and intervention.

Finding ways of recognising, and thereby creating, a demand for resources is an important aspect of practice as is ensuring that the gender perspective of women is included in all existing provisions. Individuals and groups of social workers can collect evidence of sexism and of need. Channelling information does not just have to be through the management hierarchy of social services or probation, although there may be interested senior management. If this seems doubtful or if rejection is certain, then other allies must be found so that issues of women's needs can be raised and met.

One important resource available in a growing number of local authorities is equal opportunities units and women's committees. These are valuable channels into other committees, including that responsible for social services. By defining issues as relevant to the attainment of equality on the basis of gender, sexuality, race, class or disability, the demands and needs of women can be validated. Once an issue is defined in this way, it becomes possible to argue that resources should be made available in order to implement the equal opportunities policies. This redefinition of women's needs can also validate new ways of practice in statutory social work agencies; the message goes through the management hierarchy from the top down, having first been passed laterally from one committee to another.

Where equal opportunity officers have yet to be appointed, or are grossly overworked, groups of interested women may need to do the development work, including writing documents of a style and length appropriate for the officers responsible for the equal opportunities policy to process through the authority. By joining forces with other women who are not employed by the local authority it becomes possible to speak to a range of people, including councillors, in order to explain why the issue you wish to raise is relevant to the implementation of equal opportunities policies. Even with equal opportunities policies it cannot be assumed that everyone will immediately understand the point you wish to make, but their existence makes it possible for needs and the means of meeting them to become visible.

6.   Ensuring that women are involved in the decision-making and policy-making processes of the agency

But what if a case is made and seems to be heard, but by the time resources are made available the heart of the matter seems to be lost or transformed in a way that negates your original intentions? This can happen if the decision-makers are outsiders to the project; if the largely male decision-makers begin to redefine what is needed and what is possible. However valid they may think their view is, something other than what the recipients of the service intended emerges.

Although the Seebohm Report recommended in 1968 that clients should be involved in the assessment of services provided to them, this almost never happens. Involving women clients in the decision-making and policy-making processes of statutory agencies is particularly difficult to attain because of the way professionals view their expertise and the bureaucratic nature of large scale organisations. But progress is being made and could be extended. For example, the Camden Resources and Information For Girls Project aims to evaluate statutory services (social services, health, and education), existing work with girls, and to initiate resources for girls and young women when appropriate (Pearce, 1986). Another example is that of a support group comprised of interagency workers to set up provision for Bengali girls (Chowdray, 1986).

More women are needed in the management of statutory and voluntary agencies in order to further the involvement of girls and women who are clients in monitoring, decision-making and policy formation in social services. A commitment to a woman-centred approach to social work practice must also involve finding ways of involving clients in agency processes.

7. Drawing up a code for feminist practice

In the next chapter we present the views of women who attended the courses on what should be included in a code of non-sexist practice. This is a beginning and we hope you, the reader, will find it helpful and that you will add to it, refining and developing woman-centred practice. We think drawing up a code for non-sexist and woman-centred practice is a useful strategy in achieving the reorientation of the work of colleagues, of increasing understanding about social work with women amongst the public at large and the decision-makers in local authorities and government departments and agencies, and in furthering student training.

Questions

1. In creating more manageable ways of working with women clients what do you think are the most important points to bear in mind when
   – preparing ourselves?
   – devising principles underpinning women-centred practice?
   – making our methods more gender relevant?
   – linking women clients with agencies focusing on women and their needs?
   – increasing resources for women?
   – ensuring that women are involved in the decision-making and policy-making processes of the agency?
   – drawing up a code of non-sexist women-centred practice.

2. Are these the same or additional points from those raised in the text?
3. How would you see these points turned into practical statements of intent?
4. Make a list now before turning to the next page.
5. Turn to the next page. Compare our suggestions with yours. Amend our Code of Practice to take account of your ideas.

Conclusion: A Code of Practice for Non-sexist Woman-centred Social Work

In the preceding chapters we have explained why we think the assumption that gender is not an issue in social work is both erroneous and dangerous. New policies and practices are needed to alter the balance of power between women and men as colleagues and in professional relationships with clients. We have two suggestions that we think should be adopted as goals immediately and implemented:

1. A reduction in the number of men in higher levels of decision-making hierarchies in social work. An increase in the number of women in higher levels of decision-making requires a systematic plan to reduce the number of male managers. It is essential that these plans are made alongside those aimed to increase the presentation of black people at these levels. Without this, black women will still remain doubly disadvantaged. We regard the reduction in the number of men in management to be desirable in and of itself and not simply the way the number of women can be increased.

    We are not making this recommendation because we think men or women are constitutionally incapable of change, but because gender considerations in social work organisations and service delivery are seriously disadvantaging women as clients and as workers. Overcoming institutional sexism has its parallel in overcoming racism and other divisions between people. These are consolidated by differential access to power and experienced through social institutions. Whether the differential power is located in gender, race, sexuality or social class, a solution cannot be solely located in those in power vowing to behave better.

2.   The adoption and implementation of whole agency anti-sexist policies to alter, and thereby improve relationships between men and women colleagues in direct practice and their immediate managers. Action to make both men and women social workers more gender-conscious must be directed at work both with clients and with colleagues. Policies must include procedures for monitoring and evaluating their effectiveness so that they become more than slogans or tokens of intent. Both these recommendations require a changed view of women and of the relative merits of men and women in social work organisations and in the family. Thus our proposals for a code of practice for woman-centred social work involves personal awareness as well as strategies and techniques for intervention.

Awareness

1.   Accept ourselves and women clients as women, not as the occupants of the social roles of wife, mother, carer, or adolescent girl.
2.   Be aware that identity is crucial, but that the frame of reference for our identity as women may change over time and vary between women.
3.   Be aware of the pervasiveness of sexism and how sexual stereotyping, conditioning and discrimination can affect individual women; how they see themselves, their options, behaviour, and decisions that are taken about them and us.
4.   Explore your own personal attitudes and biases about women and use your increased understanding to deal with them.
5.   Be aware of institutionalised sexism in agencies and programmes, in practice, theories and techniques.

6. Understand the links between processes, such as socialisation, with the outcome in terms of women's personal identity and gender role behaviour. Identify the changes which take place over a woman's lifetime.

7. Be aware of the nature of the survival strategies which women have developed and used. Identify the benefits and the negatives which these strategies bring to women clients and to yourself.

8. Recognise how social definitions cause women's problems. Resist pathologising women's personalities and behaviours.

9. Be aware of the complexity and often the slowness of change and that effecting change frequently means campaigning and making alliances outside the agency and the profession.

10. Be aware that working for change for women means being better than not the same as our colleagues. We need to be more skilled, better informed to be seen as competent.

11. Be aware that oppressions are often put in competition with each other for scarce resources and attention. Resist making hierarchies of what are interacting oppressions.

12. Like women and enjoy working with them. Like yourself.

Practice

1. Explore commonalities and diversities between yourself and women clients and between women clients when making assessments and during practice. Use your own experience.

2. Create situations in which social workers and clients can share and learn from each other.

3. Believe the woman client, accept her and the problem she brings.

4. Support and begin all women groups for clients and social workers which recognise diversities as well as commonalities between women.

5. Work in non-hierarchical ways with clients whenever possible. Use collective ways of working with clients and within the agency.

6. Enhance women's sense of control and coping by recognising women's strategies for coping as forms of resistance and struggle.

7. Encourage the sharing of experience, resources, strategies for coping.

8. Recognise that some strategies undermine us and women clients, and that as our lives change we have to learn new ones which will work more effectively for women clients and ourselves.

9. Encourage women to set limits to their responsibilities and to find ways with them of lifting some of the responsibilities off them. Create spaces for women even though these are small.

10. Recognise and validate the emotions expressed by women, including ourselves; they are part of our assessments, our action and our strategies rather than impediments.

11. Work with women, and the agency, in separating individual responsibility from the social and economic context in which women live.

12. The problems women bring are multi-dimensional; use the full range of social work methods with women clients; individual, group and community work. Learn to cross boundaries and make bridges within your own agency and between agencies.

13. Find out about, devise and implement women centred approaches. This includes finding out about, devising and implementing approaches which recognise the impact of racism, and that utilise understanding of culture and sexuality.

14. Share what you have learned with other workers, make good practice visible within your own agency and whenever possible more widely.

15. Check out information given to you about women clients and challenge definitions and assessments that blame the victim.

16. Find ways of working that validate women's strengths.

17. Be honest with women clients even when the news is bad. Overcoming secrecy is the way to promote accountability even when power cannot be totally shared with women clients.
18. Hand back control to women, find ways to involve women clients in decision-making and policy-making processes of the agency.
19. Work with others to increase resources for women.
20. Refer women clients to agencies that can offer empowering experiences and services thereby supplementing your work, or by providing women with an alternative resource. Agencies such as Women's Aid, Rape Crisis, Black Women's Groups, Incest Survivors' groups and Lesbian Line can identify unambiguously with women's experiences and problems.
21. Think of ways that can be used to solve problems, change situations, and improve the lives of women *now*, at the time when they need help.

References

Abramowitz, Naomi (1985) 'Status of women in Faculty and status of women's studies in Israeli Schools Of Social Work', *Social Work Education*, vol. 4, no. 3, Winter, pp. 3–6.

Ahmed, S. (1984) 'Cultural racism in work with women and girls', in *Women: Cultural Perspectives*, Transcultural Psychiatry Society. UK Workshops and Papers: Family Life, Sexism and Racism, Community Views.

Alinsky, Saul (1972) *Rules for Radicals*, New York, Vintage Books.

Allatt, Patricia; Keil, Teresa; Bryman, Alan and Bytheway, Bill (1987) *Women and the Life Cycle: Transitions and turning points*, London, Macmillan.

Allen, Sheila and Wolkowitz, Carol (1987) *Homeworking: Myths and Realities*, London, Macmillan.

Anderson, Digby and Dawson, Graham (1986) *Family Portraits*, London, The Social Affairs Unit.

Arcana, Judith (1981) *Our Mothers' Daughters*, London, The Women's Press.

Arcana, Judith (1983) *Every Mother's Son: The role of mothers in the making of men*, London, The Women's Press.

Argyle, Michael; Salter, Veronica; Nicholson, Hilary; Williams, Marilyn and Burgess, Philip (1970) 'The communication of inferior and superior attitudes by verbal and non-verbal signals', *The British Journal of Social and Clinical Psychology*, vol. 9, pp. 221–31.

Association of Community Workers (1982) *Women In Collective Action*, London, ACW.

Austerberry, H. and Watson, S. (1983) *Women on the Margins: A study of single women's housing problems*, Housing Research Group, London, City University.

Baker Miller, Jean (1976) *Towards A New Psychology of women*, Harmondsworth, Penguin.

Baldwin, Sally and Glendenning, Caroline (1983) 'Employment, women and their disabled children', in Finch, Janet and Groves, Dulcie, *Labour of Love*, London, Routledge & Kegan Paul, pp. 53–71.

Ball, Rosemary (1984) 'Thoughts on depression in Jewish families' in *Women: Cultural Perspectives*, Transcultural Psychiatry Society (UK).

Ballard, Barbara (1984) 'Women part-time workers: evidence from the 1980 women in employment survey', *Employment Gazette*, Department of Employment, September, pp. 409–16.

Barclay Report (1982) *Social Workers: Their role and tasks*, London, Bedford Square Press and NCVO.

Bayley, Michael; Seyd, Rosalind; Tennant, Allen and Simons, Ken (1984) 'What resources does the informal sector need to fulfil its role?' in the *Barclay Report, Papers from a Consultation Day*, London, National Institute for Social Work.

Beechey, Veronica (1985) 'The shape of the workforce to come', *Marxism Today*, vol. 29, no. 8.

Beechey, Veronica and Perkins, Tessa (1987). *A Matter of Hours: Women, Part-time Work & the Labour Market*, Cambridge, Polity Press.

Bell, Colin and Newby, Howard (1976) 'Husbands and wives: the dynamics of the deferential dialectic', in Leonard Barker, Diana and Allen, Sheila (eds) *Dependence and Exploitation in Work and Marriage*, London, Longman, pp. 152–68.

Bernard, Jessie (1972) *The Future Of Marriage*, New Haven, Yale University Press, 1982.

Bernardez, Teresa (1983) 'Women in Authority: Psychodynamic and interactional aspects', *Social Work with Groups*, vol. 6, no. 3/4, Fall/Winter, pp. 43–9.

Bhavnani, Reena (1987) Personal communication.

Binney, Val; Harkell, Gina and Nixon, Judy (1981) *Leaving Violent Men: A study of refuges and housing for battered women*, London: National Women's Aid Federation.

Blaxter, Mildred and Patterson, Elizabeth (1982) *Mothers and Daughters: A three generational study of health attitudes and behaviour*, London, Heinemann.

Bottoms, A. E. and McWilliams, William (1979) 'A non-treatment paradigm for probation practice', *British Journal of Social work*, vol. 9, no. 2, pp. 159–202.

Borkowski, Margaret; Murch, Mervyn and Walker, Val (1983) *Marital Violence: The Community response*, London, Tavistock.

Boulton, Mary Georgina (1983) *On Being A Mother: A study of women with pre-school children*, London, Tavistock.

Brannen, Julia and Wilson, Gail (eds) (1987) *Give and Take in Families: Studies in resource distribution*, London, Unwin Hyman.

Brent, London Borough of (1985). *A Child in Trust: The report of the enquiry into the circumstances surrounding the death of Jasmine Beckford*, London Borough of Brent Borough Council.

British Association Of Social Workers (1982) *Guidelines on Social Work Practice with Ethnic Minorities*, Birmingham, BASW.

Brook, Eve and Davis, Ann (eds) (1985) *Women: The Family and Social Work*, London, Tavistock.

Brophy, Julia and Smart, Carol (eds) (1985) *Women-In-Law: Explorations in law, family and sexuality*, London, Routledge & Kegan Paul.

Broverman, Inge, K.; Broverman, Donald; Clarkeson, Frank; Rosenkranz, Paul and Vogel, Susan (1970) 'Sex role stereotypes and clinical judgements of mental health', in Howell, Elizabeth and Bayer, Marjorie (eds) *Women and Mental Health*, New York, Basic Books, pp. 86–97.

Broverman, Inge K.; Vogel, Susan R.; Broverman, Donald M.; Clarkson, Frank E. and Rosenkrantz, Paul S. (1972) 'Sex role stereotypes: a current appraisal', *Journal Of Social Issues*, vol. 28, no. 2, pp. 59–78.

Brown, Colin (1984) *Black and White Britain: The third PSI survey*, London, Policy Studies Institute and Heinemann.

Brown, George and Harris, Tirrell (1978) *Social Origins of Depression: A study of psychiatric disorder in women*, London, Tavistock.

Brownmiller, Susan (1975) *Against Our Will: Men, Women and Rape*, Harmondsworth, Penguin, 1977.

Bryan, Beverley; Dadzie, Stella and Scafe, Suzanne (1985) *The Heart of the Race: Black women's lives in Britain*, London, Virago.

Burden, Dianne S. and Gottlieb, Naomi (eds) (1987) *The Woman Client: Providing human services in a changing world*, New York and London, Tavistock.

Callender, Claire (1985) 'Unemployment: The case for women' in Jones, Catherine and Brenton, Maria, *The Year Book of Social Policy in Britain 1984–5*, London, Routledge & Kegan Paul.

Callender, Claire (1987a) 'Women seeking work', in Fineman, Stephen (ed.) *Unemployment: Personal and social consequences*, London, Tavistock.

Callender, Claire (1987b) 'Redundancy, unemployment and poverty' in Glendinning, Caroline and Millar, Jane (eds) *Women and Poverty in Britain*, Brighton, Wheatsheaf.

Campbell, Elaine (1985) *The Childless Marriage: An exploratory study of couples who do not want children*, London, Tavistock.

Campbell, Beatrix (1987) *The Iron Ladies: Why do women vote Tory?*, London, Virago.

Campling, Jo (1981) *Images of Ourselves: women with disabilities*, London, Routledge & Kegan Paul.

Carew-Jones, Melanie and Watson, Hester (1985) *Making The Break: A practical, sympathetic and encouraging guide for women experiencing violence in their lives*, Harmondsworth, Penguin.

Carlen, Pat (1983) *Women and Imprisonment: A study in social control*, London, Routledge & Kegan Paul.

Carlen, Pat; Hicks, Jenny; O'Dwyer, Josie; Christina, Diana and Tchaikovsky, Chris (1985) *Criminal Women*, Cambridge, Polity Press.

Carlen, Pat and Worrall, Anne (eds) (1987) *Gender, Crime and Justice*, Milton Keynes, Open University.

Central Council for Education and Training in Social Work (1984) *Data on Training 1983*, London CCETSW.

Central Statistical Office (1986) *Social Trends* no 16, London, HMSO.

Chaney, Judith (1981) *Social Networks and Job Information: The situation of women who return to work*, Manchester, Equal Opportunities Commission and Social Science Research Council.

Chesler, Phyllis (1972) *Women and Madness*, New York, Avon.

Child Poverty Action Group (1987) *Poverty: The facts*, London, CPAG.

Chowdray, Jeheda (1986) 'A survey of provisions for Bengali girls on and around Bourne Estate', in *Girls in Trouble – Pack: Whose Problem? New approaches to work with young women for social work agencies*, Section 8, London, Rainer Foundation in conjunction with CCETSW and the Adolescents Project.

Cohen, Steve (1980) *You Don't Have to be a Lawyer to Help someone Being Threatened with Immediate Arrest, Detention or Expulsion under the Immigration Act*, Manchester Law Centre Immigration Handbook No. 4.

Cohen, Steve (1981) *The Thin End of the White Wedge: The new Nationality Laws, second class citizenship and the Welfare State*, Manchester Law Centre Immigration Handbook No. 5.

Cohen, Steve (1982) *From Ill Treatment To No Treatment: The new health regulations: Black people and internal controls*, Manchester Law Centre Immigration Handbook No. 6.

Cohen, Steve and Siddiqi, Nadia (1985) *What Would You Do If Your Fiancée Went to the Moon? Report of a working visit to Pakistan to investigate the cases of several Manchester residents whose fiancés/husbands have been refused entry into Britain*, The Manchester Wives & Fiancées Campaign, Manchester City Council.

Colledge, Michael (1981) *Unemployment and Health*, North Tyneside Community Health Council.

Commission For Racial Equality (1984) *Race and Council Housing in Hackney: Report of a formal investigation into the allocation of housing in the London Borough of Hackney*, London, CRE.

Community Care Supplement (1986) 'Inside sexism in social work', *Community Care*, 18 September, pp. i–viii.

Cook, Juliet and Watt, Shantu (1987) 'Racism Women and Poverty' in Glendinning, Caroline and Millar, Jane (eds) *Women and Poverty in Britain*, Brighton, Wheatsheaf.

Coveney, Lal; Jackson, Margaret; Jeffreys, Sheila; Kay, Leslie and Mahony, Pat (1984) *The Sexuality Papers: Male sexuality and the social control of women*, London, Hutchinson.

Coyle, Angela (1984) *Redundant Women*, London, The Women's Press.

Curno, Ann; Lamming, Anne; Leach, Lesley; Stiles, Jenny; Ward, Veronica; Wright, Anne and Ziff, Trisha (1982) '"Coming alive hurts": South Wales Association of Tenants' in *Women In Collective Action*, London, Association of Community Workers.

Currer, Caroline (1984) 'Pathan women in Bradford', – factors affecting mental health with particular reference to the effects of racism' *in* Aggrey W. Burke (ed.) 'Racism and Mental Illness', *International Journal of Social Psychiatry*, Spring, vol. 30 nos 1 & 2, pp. 72–6.

Curtis Report (1946) *Report of the Care of Children Committee*, Cmnd 6922, London, HMSO.

Dale, Jennifer and Foster, Peggy (1986) *Feminists and State Welfare*,

London, Routledge & Kegan Paul.

Dalla Costa, Mariarosa and James, Selma (1972) *The Power of Women and the Subversion of the Community*, Bristol, Falling Wall Press.

Dally, Ann (1982) *Inventing Motherhood: The consequences of an ideal*, London, Burnett Books.

Dalley, Gillian (forthcoming) *Ideologies of Caring: Rethinking community and collectivism*, London, Macmillan.

Daly, Mary (1978) *Gyn/Ecology: The metaethics of radical feminism*, London, The Women's Press.

David, Miriam (1983) 'The New Right in the USA and Britain: A new anti-feminist moral economy', *Critical Social Policy*, vol. 12, no. 3., Spring, pp. 31–46.

David, Miriam (1985) 'Motherhood, child care and the New Right', Lecture to the British Association for the Advancement of Science Annual Meeting, 20–30 August.

David, Miriam (1986) 'Moral and Maternal: The family in the Right' in Levitas, Ruth (ed.) *The Ideology of The New Right*, Cambridge, Polity Press.

Davis, Liane (1985) 'Female and male voices in social work', *Social work*, March–April, pp. 106–12.

Delphy, Christine (1976) 'Continuities and discontinuities in marriage and divorce', in Leonard Barker, Diana and Allen, Sheila (eds) *Sexual Divisions and Society: Process and change*, London, Tavistock, pp.76–89.

Delphy, Christine (1984) *Close to Home: A materialist analysis of women's oppression*, London, Hutchinson.

Department of Employment, (1984). *New Earnings Survey*, London.

Department of Employment, (1987) 'Ethnic Origin & Economic Status', *Employment Gazette*, London, pp. 18–29.

Department of Environment (1983) *Local Authorities and Racial Disadvantage*, Report of the Joint Government and Local Authority Association Working Group.

Department of Health and Social Security (1974) *Report of the Committee on One Parent Families*, London, HMSO, Cmnd 5629 (Finer Committee).

Department of Health and Social Security (1983) *Families on Low Incomes*, London, DHSS.

Department of Health and Social Security (1984) *Services for Under-Fives from Ethnic Minority Communities*, Inter-Departmental Consultative Group on Provisions for Under Fives, Report of a Sub-Group on Provision of Services for Under Fives from Ethnic Minority Communities, London, DHSS.

Department of Health and Social Security (1985) *Reforming Social Security*, vol. 1, Cmnd 9517, London, HMSO (Fowler Review).

Department of Health and Social Security (1986) *Decisions in Child Care*, London, HMSO.

Dex, Shirley (1987) *Women's Occupational Mobility*, London, Macmillan.

Dezalay, Yves (1976) 'French judicial ideology in working class divorce', in Leonard Barker, Diana and Allen, Sheila (eds) *Sexual Divisions and Society: Process and change*, London, Tavistock, pp. 90–107.

Dobash, R. Emerson and Dobash, Russell (1980) *Violence against Wives*, Shepton Mallet, Open Books.

Dobash, Russell; Dobash, R. Emerson and Gutteridge, Sue (1986) *The Imprisonment of Women*, Oxford, Blackwell.

Dominelli, Lena (1986) 'Father–Daughter incest: patriarchy's shameful secret', *Critical Social Policy*, issue 16, Summer, pp. 8–21.

Dowrick, Stephanie and Grundberg, Sibyl (eds) (1980) *Why Children?*, London, The Women's Press.

Dworkin, Andrea (1983) *Right-Wing Women: The politics of domesticated females*, London, The Women's Press.

Eichenbaum, Luise and Orbach, Susie (1982) *Outside In . . . Inside Out: Women's psychology, a feminist psychoanalytic approach*, Harmondsworth, Penguin.

Eichenbaum, Luise and Orbach, Susie (1983) *What Do Women Want?* London, Fontana.

Eichenbaum, Luise and Orbach, Susie (1985) *Understanding Women*, Harmondsworth, Penguin.

Department of Employment (1985) *Employment Gazette*, London, DE, September.

Department of Employment (1987) 'Ethnic origin and economic status', *Employment Gazette*, London, DE, January.

Equal Opportunities Commission (1980) *The Experience of Caring for Elderly and Handicapped Dependents*, Manchester, EOC.

Equal Opportunities Commission (1982a) *Caring for the elderly and Handicapped: Community care policies and women's lives*, Manchester, EOC.

Equal Opportunities Commission (1982b) *Who Cares for the Carers?* Manchester, EOC.

Equal Opportunities Commission (1984) *Carers and Services: A comparison of men and women caring for elderly people*, Manchester, EOC.

Equal Opportunities Commission (1985) *Women and Men in Britain: A statistical profile*, Manchester, EOC.

Ernst, Sheila and Goodison, Lucy (1981) *In Our Own Hands: A book of self-help therapy*, London, The Women's Press.

Fagin, Leonard and Little, Martin (1984) *Forsaken Families: The effect of unemployment on family life*, Harmondsworth, Penguin.

Fairbairns, Zoe (1979) *Benefits*, London, Virago.

Family Policy Studies Centre (1986) *One-Parent Families*, London, FPSC.

Farley, Lin (1980) *Sexual Shakedown: The sexual harassment of women on the job*, New York, Warner Books.

Feminist Review (1984) 'Many Voices, One Chant: Black Feminist Perspectives', no. 17, Autumn.

Fernando, Suman (1984) 'Racism as a Cause of Depression', in Burke, Aggrey (ed.), 'Racism and Mental Illness', *International Journal of*

Social Psychiatry, Spring, vol. 30, nos 1 & 2, pp. 41–9.

Finch, Janet (1983) *Married to the Job: Wives' incorporation in men's work*, London, Allen & Unwin.

Finch, Janet and Groves, Dulcie (eds) (1983) *A Labour of Love: Women, Work and Caring*, London, Routledge & Kegan Paul.

Fogarty, Michael (1971) *Women in Top Jobs: Four studies in achievement*, London, Allen & Unwin.

Frankenberg, Ronald (1966) *Communities in Britain: Social life in town and country*, Harmondsworth, Penguin.

Fritze, Karen (1982) *Just Because I Speak Cockney, They Think I'm Stupid: An application of Paulo Freire's concepts to community work with women*, London, Association of Community Workers.

Garvin, Charles and Reed, Beth Glover (1983) 'Gender issues in social group work: An overview', Social Work With Groups, Vol. 6, No. 3/4, Fall/Winter, pp. 5–18.

Gilligan, Carol (1982) *In a Different Voice: Psychological theory and women's development*, Cambridge, Mass., Harvard University Press.

General Household Survey Unit (1978) 'The changing circumstances of women 1971–76', *Population Trends*, vol. 13, pp. 17–22.

Girls In Trouble – pack (1986) Whose Problem? New approaches to work with young women for soical work agencies, London, Rainer Foundation in conjunction with CCETSW and the Adolescents Projects.

Gittens, Diana (1985) *The Family in Question: Changing households and familiar ideologies*, London, Macmillan.

Glendinning, Caroline and Millar, Jane (eds.) *Women and Poverty in Britain*, Brighton, Wheatsheaf.

Goldberg, E. Matilda and Warburton, William (1979) *Ends and Means in Social Work*, London, Allen and Unwin.

Goldner, Virginia (1985) 'Feminism and Family Therapy', *Family Process*, vol. 24, pp. 31–47.

Goode, William J. (1971) 'Force and Violence in the Family', *Journal of Marriage and the Family*, vol. 33, no. 4, pp. 624–36.

Goode, William J. (1963) *World Revolution and Family Patterns*, London, Free Press of Glencoe, Collier-Macmillan.

Gottlieb, Naomi (ed) (1980) *Alternative Social Services for Women*, New York, Columbia University Press.

Gottlieb, Naomi; Burden, Dianne; McCormick, Ruth and NiCarthy, Ginny (1983) 'The distinctive attributes of feminist groups', *Social Work with Groups*, vol. 6, no. 3/4, Fall/Winter, pp. 81–93.

Graham, Hilary (1987) 'Women's Poverty and Caring' in Glendinning, Groves, Dulcie (eds), *Labour of Love*, London, Routledge & Kegan Paul, pp. 13–30.

Graham, Hilary (1984) *Women, Health and the Family*, Brighton, Harvester Press.

Graham, Hilary (1987) 'Women's Poverty and Caring' in Glendenning, Caroline and Millar, Jane (eds) *Women and Poverty in Britain*, Brighton, Wheatsheaf.

Green, Eileen; Hebron, Sandra and Woodward, Diana (1987) 'Women, Leisure and Social Control', in Hanmer, Jalna and Maynard, Mary (eds) *Women, Violence and Social Control*, London, Macmillan, pp. 75–92.

Hadjifotiou, Nathlie (1983) *Women and Harassment at Work*, London, Pluto.

Hagen, B. H. and B. Hartung (1983) 'Managing Conflict in All-women Groups', *Social Work with Groups*, vol. 6, no. 3/4, Fall/Winter, pp. 95–104.

Hakim, Catherine (1987) 'Homeworking in Britain', *Employment Gazette*, London, Department of Employment, February.

Hakim, Catherine (1979) *Occupational Segregation*, Department of Employment Research Paper no. 9, London, Department of Employment.

Hale, Judy (1983) 'Feminism and Social Work Practice', in Jordan, Bill and Parton, Nigel (eds) *The Political Dimensions of Social Work*, Oxford, Blackwell.

Hamill, Lynne (1978) *Wives as Sole and Joint Breadwinners*, Government Economic Service Working Paper no. 15., London, HMSO.

Hanmer, Jalna (1978) 'Violence and the Social Control of Women', in Littlejohn, Gary; Smart, Barry; Wakeford, John and Yuval-Davis, Nira (eds) *Power and the State*, London, Croom Helm, pp.217–38.

Hanmer, Jalna (1979) 'Theories and Ideologies in British Community Work', *Community Development Journal*, vol. 14, no. 3, October, pp. 200–9.

Hanmer, Jalna (1983) *Violence Against Women*, Unit 15: 'The Changing Experience of Women', U221, Open University, Milton Keynes.

Hanmer, Jalna and Maynard, Mary (eds) (1987) *Women, Violence and Social Control*, London, Macmillan.

Hanmer, Jalna and Saunders, Sheila (1984) *Well-Founded Fear: A community study of violence to women*, London, Hutchinson.

Hanmer, Jalna and Saunders, Sheila (1987) *Women, Violence and Crime Prevention*, A West Yorkshire Police Authority Consultative Document.

Hanscombe, Gillian and Forster, Jackie (eds) (1982) *Rocking the Cradle: Lesbian mothers – a challenge in family living*, London, Sheba.

Hardicker, Pauline (1986) 'A Personal Voyage into Issues of Women and Social Work', Paper given at the Women and Social Work Conference, Ruskin College.

Hare-Mustin, R. T. (1978) 'A Feminist Approach to Family Therapy', *Family Process*, vol. 17, pp. 181–93.

Harris, Robert (1980) 'A Changing Service: The case for separating care and control in probation practice', *British Journal of Social Work*, vol. 10, no. 1, pp. 163–84.

Harrison, Mary (1987) Personal Communication.

Heidensohn, Francis (1985) *Women and Crime*, London, Macmillan.

Hemmings, Susan (ed.) (1985) *A Wealth of Experience: The lives of older women*, London, Pandora Press.

Hennig, Margaret and Jardin, Anne (1979) *The Managerial Woman*, London, Pan Books.

Henriques, Fernando; Dennis, Norman and Slaughter, Clifford (1956) *Coal is Our Life: An analysis of a Yorkshire Mining Community*, London, Tavistock, 2nd ed. 1969.

Hilberman, Elaine (1980) 'Overview: the "wife beater's wife" reconsidered', *American Journal of Psychiatry*, vol. 137, pp. 1336–47.

Hill, John Michael (1977) *The Social and Psychological Impact of Unemployment*, London, Tavistock.

Holland, Janet (1980) *Work and Women*, London, University of London Institute of Education.

Hollis, Florence (1965) *Casework: A psychosocial therapy*, New York, Random House.

Home Affairs Select Committee (1981) *Report on Racial Disadvantage*, London, HMSO.

Home Office (1986) 'The Ethnic Origins of Prisoners: The prison population on 30 June 1985 and persons received, July 1984–March 1985', *Statistical Bulletin*, London, Home Office.

Holman, Robert (1980) *Inequalities in Child Care*, London, CPAG and Family Rights Group.

Homer, Marjorie; Leonard, Anne and Taylor, Pat (1984) *Public Violence Private Shame: A report on the circumstances of women leaving domestic violence in Cleveland*, Middlesbrough, Cleveland, Cleveland Council For Voluntary Service.

Housing Services Advisory Group (1978) *The Housing of One-Parent Families*, London, Department of Environment.

Howe, David (1986) 'The Segregation of Women and Their Work in the Personal Social Services', *Critical Social Policy*, Winter.

Howell, Elizabeth and Bayer, Marjorie (eds) (1981) *Women and Mental Health*, New York, Basic Books.

Hudson, Annie (1985) 'Feminism and Social Work: Resistance of dialogue', *British Journal of Social Work*, vol. 15, pp. 635–55.

Hudson, Annie (1986) 'Troublesome Girls: Towards alternative definitions and strategies', in *Girls In Trouble — Whose Problem? New Approaches to work with young women for social work agencies*, London, Rainer Foundation in conjunction with CCETSW and the Adolescents Projects.

Hughes, John (1985) 'Some Regional Dimensions of Regional Inequality', *Labour Market Issues* no. 6, Trade Union Research Unit, Oxford, Ruskin College.

Hunt, Audrey (1970) *The Home Help Service in England and Wales*, London, HMSO.

Hunt, Audrey (1975) *Management Attitudes and Practice Towards Women at Work*, London, HMSO.

Hutter, Bridget and Williams, Gillian (eds) (1981) *Controlling Women: The normal and the deviant*, London, Croom Helm.

Inner London Education Authority (1983) *A Policy For Equality: Race*, London, ILEA Publications.

Jeffreys, Sheila (1985) *The Spinster and Her Enemies: Feminism and Sexuality 1880–1930*, London, Pandora Press.

Jones, Chris (1983) *State Social Work and the Working Class*, London, Macmillan.

Kadushin, Alfred (1976) 'Men in a Women's Profession', *Social Work*, vol. 21, pp. 440–7.

Kinsey, Alfred; Wardell, Pomeroy; Martin, Clyde and Gebhard, Paul (1953) *Sexual Behaviour in the Human Female*, Philadelphia, W. B. Saunders.

Land, Hilary (1976) 'Women: Supporters or Supported?', in Leonard Barker, Diana and Allen, Sheila (eds) *Sexual Divisions and Society: Process and change*, London, Tavistock, pp. 108–32.

Land, Hilary (1978) 'Who Cares for the Family?', *Journal of Social Policy*, vol. 7, no. 3, pp. 257–84.

Land, Hilary (1983) 'Poverty and Gender: The distribution of resources within the family', in Brown, Muriel (ed.) *The Structure of Disadvantage*, London, Heinemann, pp. 49–71.

Land, Hilary (1986) *Women and Economic Dependency*, Equal Opportunities Commission, Manchester.

Lawrence, Marilyn (1984) *The Anorexic Experience*, London, The Women's Press.

LeGrand, Julian (1982) *The Strategy of Equality*, London, Allen & Unwin.

Leonard Barker, Diana (1978) 'The Regulation of Marriage: Repressive benevolence', in Littlejohn, Gary; Smart, Barry; Wakeford, John and Yuval-Davis, Nira (eds) *Power and the State*, London, Croom Helm, pp. 239–66.

Leonard Barker, Diana (1980) *Sex and Generation: A study of courtship and weddings*, London, Tavistock.

Levie, Hugo; Gregory, Dennis and Lorentzen, Nick (1984) *Fighting Closures: Deindustrialisation and the Trade Unions 1979–1983*, Nottingham, Spokesman,

Levitas, Ruth (ed.) (1986) *The Ideology of the New Right*, Oxford, Polity Press.

Lorde, Audre (1984) *Sister Outsider*, Trumansburg, New York, Crossing Press.

Lorde, Audre (1981) 'An Open Letter to Mary Daly' in Moraga, Cherrie and Anzaldua, Gloria (eds) *A Bridge Called My Back: Writings of radical women of color*, New York, Kitchen Table Press, pp. 94–7.

The London Rape Crisis Centre (1984) *Sexual Violence: The reality for women*, London, The Women's Press.

Low Pay Unit (1987) *Low Pay Review*, no. 29, London, Low Pay Unit.

MacDonald, Barbara, with Rich, Cynthia (1984) *Look Me In The Eye: Old women, ageing and ageism*, London, Women's Press.

McKechnie, Sheila and Wilson, Des (1986) *Homes Above All Shelter*, London, Shelter.

McKee, Lorna and O'Brien, Margaret (eds) (1983) 'Taking Gender Seriously', in Gamarinkow, Eva; Morgan, David; Purvis, June and

Taylorson, Daphne (eds) *The Public and the Private*, London, Heinemann, pp. 147–61.

McKinnon, Catherine (1979) *Sexual Harassment of Working Women: A case of sex discrimination*, New Haven, Yale University Press.

McLeod, Eileen (1982) *Women Working: Prostitution Now*, London, Croom Helm.

McLeod, Eileen and Dominelli, Lena (1982) 'The Personal and the Apolitical: Feminism and moving beyond the integrated methods approach', in Bailey, Roy and Lee, Phil (eds) *Theory and Practice in Social Work*, Oxford, Basil Blackwell, pp. 112–27.

McNeill, Pearlie; McShea, Marie and Parmar, Pratibha (eds) (1987) *Through the Break, Women In Personal Struggle*, London, Sheba.

McRobbie, Angela and McCabe, Trisha (eds) (1981) *Feminism For Girls: An adventure story*, London, Routledge & Kegan Paul.

Malos, Ellen (1980) *The Politics of Housework*, London, Allison & Bushby.

Mander, Anica and Rush, Anne (1974) *Feminism As Therapy*, Toronto, Random House.

Marchant, Helen and Wearing, Betsy (eds) (1986) *Gender Reclaimed: Women in social work*, Marickville, New Zealand: Hale & Leimonger.

Martin, Jean and Roberts, Ceridwen (1984a) *Women and Employment: A life-time perspective*, Report of the 1980 DE and OPCS Women and Employment Survey, London, HMSO.

Martin, Jean and Roberts, Ceridwen (1984b) 'Women's Employment in the 1980's, *Employment Gazette*, London, DE, May.

Martin, Roderick and Wallace, Judith (1984) *Working Women in Recession: Employment, redundancy and unemployment*, Oxford, Oxford University Press.

Mayall, Berry and Petrie, Pat (1983) *Childminding and Day Nurseries: What kind of care?*, London, Heinemann.

Maynard, Mary (1985) 'The Response of Social Workers to Domestic Violence', in Pahl, Jan (ed.) *Private Violence and Public Policy: The needs of battered women and the response of the public services*, London, Routledge & Kegan Paul, pp. 125–41.

Mayo, Marjorie (1977) *Women in the Community*, London, Routledge & Kegan Paul.

Moraga, Cherrie and Anzaldua, Gloria (eds) (1981) *This Bridge Called My Back: Writings of radical women of color*, New York, Kitchen Table Press.

Morrell, Carolyn (1981) 'Weaving A Feminist Social Work Practice: The experience of Womenfocus', *Focus on Women: Journal of Addictions and Health*, no. 1, vol. 2, Spring, pp. 38–47.

Morrell, Carolyn (1987) 'Cause is Function: Towards a Feminist Model of Integration for Social Work', *Social Service Review*, March, pp. 144–55.

Morgan, David (1987) 'Masculinity and Violence' in Hanmer, Jalna and Maynard, Mary (eds) *Women, Violence and Social Control*, London, Macmillan, pp. 180–92.

Mount, Ferdinand (1982) *The Subversive Family: An alternative history of love and marriage*, London, Cape and Unwin Counterpoint.

Nairne, Kathy and Smith, Gerrilyn (1984) *Dealing With Depression*, London, The Women's Press.

National Council For One Parent Families (1983) *A Submission to the House of Commons Select Committee Inquiry into Child Care*, London, NCOPF.

National Union of Teachers and Equal Opportunities Commission (1980) *Promotion and the Women Teacher*, March.

Nelson, Sarah (1987) *Incest: Fact and Myth*, Edinburgh, Stramullion.

New, Caroline and David, Miriam (1985) *For the Children's Sake: Making child care more than women's business*, Harmondsworth, Penguin.

NiCarthy, Ginny; Merriam, Karen and Coffman, Sandra (1984) *Telling It Out: A guide to groups for abused women*, Seattle, Washington, The Seal Press.

NiCarthy, Ginny; Fuller, Addei; Stoops, Nan (1987) 'Battering and Abuse of Women, in Intimate Relationships' in Burden, Dianne and Gottlieb, Naomi (eds) *The Woman Client*, London, Tavistock.

Numa, Sharon (1985) 'Some Issues Affecting Afro-Carribbean Women', in *Women's Cultural Perspectives*, Transcultural Psychiatry Society (UK).

Oakley, Ann (1974) *The Sociology of Housework*, London, Martin Robertson, 2nd ed., Oxford, Blackwell, 1985.

Oakley, Ann (1981) *Subject Woman*, London, Martin, Robertson.

Office of Population Censuses and Surveys (1980) *Labour force Survey 1979*, London, HMSO.

Office of Population Censuses and Surveys (1985) *Labour Force Survey 1984*, London, HMSO

Oliver, Michael (1983) *Social Work with Disabled People*, London, Macmillan.

Osborne, K. (1983) 'Women in Families: Feminist therapy and family systems', *Journal of Family Therapy*, vol. 5, pp. 1–9.

Pahl, Jan (ed.) (1985) *Private Violence and Public Policy: The needs of battered women and the response of the public services*, London, Routledge and Kegan Paul.

Pahl, Jan (1980) 'Patterns of Money Management', *Journal of social Policy*, vol. 9, no. 3, pp. 313–15.

Pahl, Jan (1982) *The Allocation of Money and the Structuring of Inequality Within Marriage*, Health Services Research Unit, University of Kent, Canterbury.

Parker, Roy (1985) 'A Review of Social Work Related Research: An outline for the future', in Wedge, Peter (ed.) *Social Work Research into Practice*, Proceedings of the First Annual JUC/BASW Conference, London, September.

Parker, Roy (1981) 'Tending and Social Policy', in Goldberg, E. Matilda and Hatch, Stephen (eds), *A New Look at the Personal Social Services*, Discussion Paper no. 4, London, Policy Studies Institute.

Parsloe, Phyllida and Stevenson, Olive (1978) *Social Service Teams: A practitioner's view*, London, HMSO.

Pascall Gillian (1986) *Social Policy: A feminist analysis*, London, Tavistock.

Pattullo, Polly (1983) *Judging Women*, London, National Council For Civil Liberties.

Pearce, Jenny (1986) 'Working With Girls Researching Establishing the need', in *Girls In Trouble — Pack, Whose Problem? New approaches to work with young women for social work agencies*, Section 5, London, Rainer Foundation in conjunction with CCETSW and the Adolescents Projects.

Penfold, P. Susan and Walker, Gillian A. (1984) *Women and the Psychiatric Paradox*, Milton Keynes, Open University Press.

Pennell, Joan and Allen, David (1984) 'Personal Self, Professional Self And The Women's Movement', *Atlantis*, vol. 9, no. 2, Spring, pp. 50–8.

Popay, Jennie; Rimmer, Lesley and Rossister, Chris (1982) 'One Parent Families and Unemployment', *Employment Gazette*, December, pp. 531–5.

Popay, Jennie; Rimmer, Lesley and Rossiter, Chris (1983) *One Parent Families: Parents, children and public policy*, London, Study Commission of the Family.

Popplestone, Ruth (1980) 'Top Jobs for Women: Are the cards stacked against them?', *Social Work Today*, 23 September, pp. 12–15.

Popplestone, Ruth (1981) 'A Women's Profession', unpublished paper.

Pringle, Mia Kellmer (1975) 'Setting The Scene', *Concern*, no. 17, Summer, p. 8.

Pringle, Mia Kellmer (1980) *The Needs of Children*, London, Hutchinson.

Radford, Jull (1987) 'Policing Male Violence – Policing women', in Hanmer, Jalna and Maynard, Mary (eds) *Women, Violence and Social Control*, London, Macmillan, pp. 30–45.

Raymond, Janice (1986) *A Passion for Friends*, London, The Women's Press.

Reed, Beth Glover (1983) 'Women Leaders in Small Groups', *Social Work with Groups*, vol. 6, nos. 3/4, Fall/Winter, pp. 35–42.

Report of the Review Panel (1986) *A Different Reality: An account of black people's experiences and their grievances before and after the Handsworth rebellion of September 1985*, Birmingham, West Midlands Council.

Rhodes, Dusty and McNeill, Sandra (eds) (1985) *Women Against Violence Against Women*, London, Only Women Press.

Rich, Adrienne (1977) *Of Woman Born: Motherhood as experience and institution*, London, Virago.

Rich, Adrienne (1980) 'Compulsory Heterosexuality and Lesbian Existence', *SIGNS*, vol. 5, no. 4, pp. 631–60.

Richards, Margaret (1987) 'Developing the Content of Practice Teaching', *Social Work Education*, vol. 6, no. 2, pp. 4–9.

Rieker, Patricia Perri and Carmen, Elaine Hilberman (1986) 'The Victim-To-Patient Process: The disconfirmation and transformation of abuse', *American Journal of Orthopsychiatry*, vol. 56, no. 3, July, p. 360–70.

Rights of Women Lesbian Custody Group (1986) *Lesbian Mothers' Legal*

Handbook, London, The Women's Press.

Rights of Women (1984) *Lesbian Mothers on Trial: A report on lesbian mothers and child custody*, London, Rights of women (52/54 Featherstone Street, London EC1Y 8RT).

Riley, Denise (1983) *War in the Nursery: Theories of the child and mother*, London, Virago.

Rimmer, Lesley (1983) 'The Economics of Work and Caring', in Finch, Janet and Groves, Dulcie (eds) *Labour of Love*, London, Routledge & Kegan Paul.

Rutter, Michael (1981) *Maternal Deprivation Reassessed*, Harmondsworth, Penguin.

Scott, Hilda (1984) *Working Your Way to the Bottom: The feminisation of poverty*, London, Pandora Press.

Schaeffer, Rudolph (1977) *Mothering*, London, Fontana/Open Books.

Scruton, Roger (1980) *The Meaning of Conservatism*, Harmondsworth, Penguin.

Sears, Maureen (1986) personal communication.

Sedley, Ann and Benn, Melissa (1982) *Sexual Harassment at Work*, London, National Council For Civil Liberties.

Seebohm Report (1968) *Report of the Committee on Local Authority and Allied Personal Social Services*, Cmnd 3703, London, HMSO.

Select Committee on Violence in the Family (1975) vol. I (together with Proceedings of the Committee), vol. II Evidence, vol. III Appendices, London, HMSO.

Seligman, Martin (1975) *Helplessness: On depression, development and death*, San Francisco, Freeman.

Shifra (1986) 'Jewish Women's Aid: A Northern support and counselling service', nos. 3 & 4, December, p. 60.

Short Report (1984) *Report of Commons Social Services Committee on Children in Care*, London, HMSO.

Shimmin, Syliva; McNally, Joyce and Liff, Sonia (1981) 'Pressures on Women Engaged in Factory Work', *Employment Gazette*, August, pp. 344–9.

Sinfield, Adrian (1981) *What Unemployment Means*, Oxford, Martin Robertson.

Smart, Carol (1984) *The Ties That Bind: Law, marriage and the reproduction of patriarchal relations*, London, Routledge & Kegan Paul.

Smith, Barbara and Smith, Beverly (1981) 'Across the Kitchen Table: sister to sister dialogue' in Moraga, Charrie and Anxaldua, Gloria (eds) *This Bridge Called My Back: Writing of radical women of color*, New York, Kitchen Table Press, pp. 113–27.

Smith, Richard (1987) *Unemployment & Health*, Oxford, Oxford University Press.

Social Service Inspectorate (1986) *Inspection of the Supervision of social Workers in the Assessment of Monitoring of Cases of Child Abuse When Children Subject to a Court Order Have Been Returned Home*, London, DHSS.

Solomon, Barbara Bryant (1987) 'Empowerment: Social work in oppressed communities', *Journal of Social Work Practice*, vol. 2, no. 4, p. 79–91.

Solomon, Barbara Bryant (1976) *Black Empowerment: Social work with oppressed communities*, New York, Columbia University Press.

Spender, Dale (1980) *Man Made Language*, London, Routledge & Kegan Paul.

Stanko, Elizabeth (1985) *Intimate Intrusions: Women's experience of male violence*, London, Routledge & Kegan Paul.

Stark, Evan; Flitcraft, Anne and Frazier, W. (1979) 'Medicine and Patriarchial Violence: The social construction of a "private" event', *International Journal of Health Services*, vol. 9, no. 3, pp. 461–92.

Statham, Daphne (1978) *Radicals In Social Work*, London, Routledge & Kegan Paul.

Study Commission on the Family (1983) *Families in the Future*, London, Study Commission on the Family.

Sutherland, Ian (1987) 'To Heat or Eat', *Community Care*, 2 April, pp. 12–13.

Sutton, Carol (1979) *Psychology for Social Workers and Counsellors: An introduction*, London, Routledge & Kegan Paul.

Thatcher, Margaret (1983) 'Facing the New Challenge' in Ungerson, Clare (ed.) *Women and Social Policy: A reader*, London, Macmillan, pp. 213–17.

Townsend, Peter (1979) *Poverty In the UK*, Harmondsworth, Penguin.

Turner, Frank (1986) 'Conference Summary', Clinical Social Work in a Turbulent world, *Journal of Social Work Practice*, vol. 2, no. 4, pp. 150–1.

Ungerson, Clare (ed.) (1985) *Women and Social Policy: A reader*, London, Macmillan.

Ungerson, Clare (1983) 'Women and Caring: Skills tasks and taboos', in Garmanikow, Eva; Morgan, David; Purvis, June and Taylorson, Daphne (eds) *The Public and the Private*, London, Heinemann, pp. 62–77.

Walby, Christine (1987) 'Why Are There So Few Women Working in Senior Management Positions?', *Social Work Today*, 16 February, pp. 10–11.

Walker, Alan (1987) 'The Poor Relation: poverty among older women', in Glendenning, Caroline and Millar, Jane (eds) *Woman and Poverty in Britain*, Brighton, Wheatsheaf.

Walker, Alice (1984) *In Search of Our Mother's Gardens*, London, The Women's Press.

Walton, Ronald (1975) *Women in Social Work*, London, Routledge & Kegan Paul.

Ward, Elizabeth (1984) *Father–Daughter Rape*, London, The Women's Press.

Wells, Owen (1983) *Promotion and the Woman Probation Officer*, London, National Association of Probation Officers.

Welsh Women's Aid (1980) *Mrs. Hobson's Choice: A survey of the employment position of women who have been through Women's Aid refuges in South Wales*, Cardiff, Welsh Women's Aid.

Whitehead, Ann (1976) 'Sexual Antagonism in Herefordshire', in Leonard Barker, Diana and Allen, Sheila (eds) *Dependence and Exploitation in Work and Marriage*, London, Longman, pp. 169–203.

Wilkin, D. (1979) *Caring For the Mentally Handicapped Child*, London, Croom Helm.

Wilkinson, Sue (ed.) (1986) *Feminist Social Psychology: Developing theory and practice*, Milton Keynes, Open University Press.

Wilson, Amrit (1978) *Finding a Voice: Asian women in Britain*, London, Virago.

Wilson, Elizabeth (1977) *Women and the Welfare State*, London, Tavistock.

Wilson, Elizabeth (1980) 'Feminism and Social Work', in Brake, Mike and Bailey Roy (eds) *Radical Social Work and Practice*, London, Edward Arnold.

Wilson, Elizabeth (1983) *What is to be Done about Violence to Women? Crisis in the eighties*, Harmondsworth, Penguin.

Wise, Sue (1985) 'Becoming a Feminist Social Worker', *Studies in Sexual Politics*, no. 6, University of Manchester.

Women, Immigration and Nationality Group (1985) *Women, Immigration and Nationality*, London, Pluto.

Women in MIND (1986) *Finding Our Own Solutions: Women's experience of mental health care*, London, MIND.

Women's National Commission (1981) *Report on Homelessness Amongst Women*, London, Cabinet Office.

Women's Aid Federation England Research Group (1984) 'Positive Proposals for Research from Women's Aid Federation England', in Hanmer, Jalna and Saunders, Sheila *Well-Founded Fear: A community study of violence to women*, London, Hutchinson, pp. 86–100.

Wright, Fay (1983) 'Single Carers: Employment, housework and caring', in Finch, Janet and Groves, Dulcie (eds), *Labour of Love*, London, Routledge & Kegan Paul, pp. 89–105.

Index

All references are to women unless otherwise specified.

164   *Index*

166   *Index*